Pearls of Wisdom
LIFE SKILLS STRATEGIES **BY ALLAN SEALY**

DELUXE EDITION

COMMUNICATING EXCELLENCE

Copyright © 2016 Allan Sealy

All rights reserved. No part of this publication may be produced, distributed, or transmitted in any form or by any means, including photocopying, recording, or other electronic or mechanical methods, without the prior written permision of the publisher, except in the case of brief quotations embodied in critical reviews and certain other noncommercial uses permitted by copyright law.

For permission requests, write to the publisher, addressed "Attention: Permissions Coordinator" at the email address below:

Life and Success Media Ltd

Email: info@abookinsideyou.com   Website: www.abookinsideyou.com

Unless otherwise stated, all scriptural references are taken from the New King James Version of the Bible. Other versions cited are NIV, NKJV, AMP and KJV. Quotations marked NIV are taken from the HOLY BIBLE, NEW INTERNATIONAL VERSION. Copyright © 1973, 1978, 1984 by International Bible Society. Used by permission of Hodder and Stoughton Ltd, a member of the Hodder Headline Plc Group. All rights reserved. "NIV" is a registered trademark of International Bible Society. UK trademark number 1448790. Quotations marked KJV are from the Holy Bible, King James Version.

Pearls of Wisdom Life Skills Strategies
ISBN: 978-1-907402-97-5

Pearls of Wisdom Life Mastery Website:
www.allansealy.com

DEDICATION

This Book is dedicated to
my daughters, Jasmin & Jada.
I love you both deeply.

SPECIAL THANKS

I want to give special thanks to:

My Father (The Wise One)
- for your wisdom, love and guidance -

My Mother (My Rock)
- for your unfailing love and sacrifice -

Bishop Dr. Wayne Malcolm (The Entrepreneurs Pastor)
- thank you for your vision -

CONTENTS

PREFACE [7]
INTRODUCTION [21]

Self Mastery Series

Exposing Hardness of Heart [25]
It's Time To Get Extreme [41]
Living With Dirt [51]
Passion Killers [59]

Faith Series

Perception [73]
Overcoming The Fear of Failure [79]
Manifesting The Promise [87]
Strong Faith [95]
Heaven's Master Key [101]

CONTENTS

The Kingdom Series

Kingdom 101	[111]
Greater Than My Roots	[117]
Discovering Your Hidden Treasure	[145]
Keys To Kingdom Promotion	[157]
A Call To Repentance	[165]

Personal Power Series

A Winning Perspective	[173]
Breaking Mental Barriers	[179]
The Power of Focus	[191]
The Power of Choice	[201]
The Need for Integrity	[211]
Developing A Spirit of Excellence	[223]
More Than A Conqueror	[229]
Fit For Abundance	[237]

*It is the glory of God to conceal a thing
but the glory of Kings to search things out*

PREFACE
LET THERE BE LIGHT

It has been 18 years since I made the decision to follow my passion for art. This decision was made having just completed 7 years of arduous study in electronics, culminating in a Bachelors degree in Electronic engineering. You may ask, "why spend so many years studying electronics only to embark on a career in art?"

Well, to begin with, I have always been passionate about art and spent much of my childhood drawing and painting. I had every intention on becoming an artist by profession, only to be told by my school teacher that I would not be able to make a living from art, despite my talent. This was devastating for me, especially as it came from my *art teacher*. I have always been ambitious and the thought of struggling to make money from art did not rest well with me. As an alternative, I decided to pursue a career in electronics, despite my dislike

◆PREFACE

for maths. It was a subject I found interesting and it seemed a more stable profession. When I finally got to University, having completed the necessary college courses, the UK was experiencing a recession which prevented me and the other students from getting the 12 months work experience placement that was integral to the course. Thus I obtained my degree forgoing crucial work experience that would have endowed me with valuable practical skills - *to this day, I couldn't fix a kettle if my life depended on it*. Undeterred, I went into the big wide world determined to get a job in electronics and start my meteoric climb to the top (whatever that was). After a year of receiving rejection letters, anxiety had all but eaten away my optimism.

I decided to take up art again (after a 7 year hiatus), more for therapeutic reasons than anything else. I worked on unfinished sketches I had started way back when. It didn't take long for that overwhelming and somewhat addictive enthusiasm for art to return. Hours of drawing replaced looking for a job, a luxury I could well afford as I was still living under my parent's roof.

My mother's home was a hub for many of her fellow church members, eager to taste her renowned Caribbean cuisines. As a result of these many visits to the house, my artwork soon came to the attention of the pastor. I must have made an impression, as I was asked by one of church deacons to design a flier for the church's upcoming convention. Soon after, other pastors sought my handiwork and I gladly did it (for next to nothing) as I relished the novelty of someone wanting me to design for them. It was then that I began to explore the possibility of actually becoming a freelance graphic designer. Meanwhile, under the guidance of my cousin (who had a relatively lucrative career as an electrical engineer), significant steps had been made to set me up as a telecommunications engineer. It was at this juncture that I was faced with the dilemma of which path I should take. My passion and gift was art, but I was reluctant to turn my back on electronics after 7 years of study. I was stuck at a crossroad, looking for direction.

The answer came when I attended a seminar held by a Bahamian Pastor named Dr. Myles Munroe, who at that time (early 90's) was relatively unknown in the UK. He was speaking about releasing your potential and it was at one of his break-out sessions that I heard these life changing words:

> *"Your gifts and talents are an indication of your purpose"*

Those words blew my young mind on different levels. First of all, the concept of a divine purpose for my life was completely foreign to me. Did I lack ambition? Certainly not! However, the idea of 'God' having a plan and purpose for my life was not something I had

PREFACE

ever considered. Added to that, what seemed to be my only gift at the time was art, and I could not see how or why a hobby, that at best could be used to earn a living, should play any part in some divine plan and purpose. That in itself implied that my talent was more than just my own personal interest; it was something given to me on purpose, for a purpose. That day I experienced a paradigm shift and began to see things from a totally different perspective. If God indeed had a purpose for my life, then to do anything else would be meaningless. From then on I became 'purpose driven' and went on to see the importance of following one's passion, as it emanates from one's purpose and destiny. When I left that meeting my dilemma had vanished; I would follow the path that art was leading me to.

One other thing I learnt that day, was the biblical concept of light and darkness. Simply put, knowledge is light and ignorance is darkness.

Walking in the light

Light is that which enables one to see. Knowledge is light because what you see is determined literally by what you know. This is because sight is a faculty of the mind, not the eyes. Your eyes serve only as the window that gives entrance to the streams of images you encounter every passing second. It is your mind that interprets and gives meaning to those images. Just think how you might react to seeing a tree for the first time and not know what it was. That tree might appear very threatening to you. Thus, ignorance gives entrance to fear, and when we are fearful we act in a manner that ultimately serves to debilitate us. Historically speaking, we tend to destroy what we don't understand.

Ignorance truly is darkness as it blinds us from the truth about ourselves and also prevents us from seeing solutions and recognizing opportunities. The inability to see lies at the root of our problems; however, as quickly as darkness disappears when light is shone, problems will vanish when the triune power of knowledge, wisdom and understanding shines bright. You may view that statement as idealistic or even utopian, however, real solutions evade us when we dismiss life's simple truths. What you don't know IS hurting you. Hence the bible urges us to walk in the light and not in darkness. In order to do so, we must understand one of the most important aspects of light.

Light is usually thought of in terms of brilliance, luminance or brightness. We think of sources of light such as sunlight or moonlight (which is reflected sunlight), light from a fireplace or a light bulb. In scientific terms, light from these sources are known as 'white' or 'visible' light. It is the combination of the spectrum of colours we see. Imagine being in a windowless room with the

♦PREFACE

lights turned off; leaving you in complete darkness. Imagine also that light for that room being controlled by a dimmer switch. If you only turn the switch slightly, the light will come on, but not enough to give you a full view of the room. As a result, there will be parts or details of the room that you could not see. Even the color of the wall may not be discernible. As you turn the switch more, the room becomes brighter and you will be able to see more of it. When you turn the switch fully on, you will be able to see the room in it's entirety: the door, the ceiling and all the contents. You will be able to see if the room is tidy or disorganized, whether it is in good condition or in need of repair. Basically you will be able to see the *appearance* of your surroundings.

What you won't be able to see, however, is beyond the walls of the room because the walls are opaque. They are opaque only because white light cannot pass through or penetrate the walls. As our eyes are attuned only to the frequency range of white light, we are limited to what white light can reveal. Simply put, if white light could penetrate walls then we will be able to see through *walls*.

Apart from white light, there are other forms of light in coexistence such as ultraviolet, infra red, gamma rays and x-rays. These lights are not visible to the naked eye because they exist outside the range of frequencies our eyes can detect. Most of us will be familiar with the use of X-ray machines used in hospitals. X-ray machines are used to acquire an 'X-ray image' of the inside of an object. Unlike white light, x-rays are able to penetrate objects that are opaque to us. X-ray machines make it possible for us to see the inside of an object because they have an image detection system that enable us to see the images reflected by X-rays. If our eyes were attuned to the frequencies of X-rays we will be able to see through objects without the aid of an x-ray machine.

Thus, the true power of light is not measured in how bright it shines, but in it's ability to allow us to see through *barriers*. If we go back to our imaginary room, the brightest flood light within that room would not allow us to see through it's walls. The very character of white light makes it impossible. All it is able to do is shed light on your surroundings.

Knowledge works by the same principle. The power of the knowledge you have is determined by it's ability to allow you to see beyond barriers. When I speak of barriers, I am referring to those that hinder what we could know. Barriers like distance, time, perspective, environment, experience, miseducation and even deception. For example, I could not effectively advise anyone experiencing a particular challenge in their life purely based on face value. To do that, I would have to give what I call a 'white light' viewpoint which is an opinion based purely on appearance. To give effective advice, I would need the benefits of insight, oversight, experience, education and empathy. Thus, it is the *source* of information that determines it's effectiveness.

The How's and The Why's

That being said, we live in a world that relies on science to shed light on how everything works. Be that as it may, science can only provide information derived from the behavior of the physical and natural world. The natural world is the realm of manifestation. It is the world you can see, rooted in a world that you cannot see (spiritual). When we look at a plant, we know there is more to it than what we can see. We know that plant has roots hidden under the earth. This is a simple analogy of the relationship between the spiritual and natural realm; the seen coexisting with the unseen. The natural world is the manifestation of things spiritual. Thus, things seen (physical) are brought about by things unseen (spiritual).

By only studying the physical world, we can discover how things work, but only speculate on why something works. Understanding 'how' things work is good and practical, however, understanding 'why' something works is essential if we are to avoid it's abuse. When you don't know the purpose of a thing, abuse of it is inevitable.

We are both spiritual and physical in nature and we live in a natural world that co-exists with a spiritual world. That is the duality of our reality. One is not independent of the other. If we neglect our spiritual needs and nature we create an adverse impact on our physical nature. That being said, it is important to understand what truly motivates us, as motives and purpose express and fulfil a spiritual need. This fact leads to a profound but simple truth:

> *"how you live is determined
> by why you live"*

This simple truth is key to effective living. Nothing is achieved without motive or purpose. Despite the multitudes of worthy causes that exist in this world, if our motives are not rooted in God - the purpose giver and source of all things, then we will inevitably verge from the reason of our very existence.

If your belief system rests entirely on scientific knowledge, you will never determine the 'why' of your existence. Your life will be about 'how was this done,' instead of knowing 'why.' Knowing why puts you on the cutting edge and is the hallmark of leadership.

◆PREFACE

Spiritual Insight

As mentioned, the power of the knowledge you have is determined by its ability to allow you to see beyond barriers. Scientific knowledge will not allow you to see beyond the barrier of this natural realm. To put things in perspective, I am not adverse to science; after all, it is the study of God's creation. However, the conflict between science and faith is due only to scientific *theories*, not science itself. Science alone cannot provide the answers we seek to our internal questions. These questions must be answered if we are to live according to our true nature. To this end we must seek another trusted source of light: one that will endow us with spiritual insight and allow us to see beyond all barriers, even the passage of time (prophetic). Spiritual insight will put you at the helm of your life and enable you to effectively determine your future.

That is what it did for me as I embraced those simple but life changing words that gave context and direction to my life. Since then, I have allowed spiritual insight, derived from biblical principles, to be my trusted source for guidance and my reference for truth. It is the principles and lessons of God's word, that has allowed me to break through barriers that others said I could not cross. Following my passion for art has been a journey of self discovery, personal growth and a deepened faith in God. I have experienced business success and received many accolades. I have also endured and overcome many personal and professional challenges. My passion for art gave me a deep appreciation for excellence and as I embraced and strived for excellence in all areas of my life, I discovered a hidden passion - a passion to help others succeed. Thus, despite being described as painfully shy as a teenager, my passion has forced me out of the comfort of working behind the scenes and compelled me to coach, speak and teach in many public arenas. My best is still yet to come and I believe yours is too!

Becoming Attuned

As previously stated, the human eye is attuned only to the frequencies of white light. If it were possible for our eyes to detect the frequencies of x-rays, we would be able to see through objects without the aid of an X-ray machine. In like manner, we have to be attuned to the light of God's word in order to acquire spiritual insight. Becoming attuned to the *frequencies* of God's word requires faith. His word is not readily discernible without faith. That is why faith is key to all biblical teaching. The reason you must have faith is because you have to be willing to act on knowledge that is beyond how things may appear. You have to put your trust in information that is not readily proven by scientific or physical evidence. That is why spirituality seems foolish

◆PREFACE

to those who act only on what their five senses can tell them. However, you will be surprised by the array of people who occupy the upper echelons of society who owe their success to acts of faith.

The decision I made to follow my passion was based on information that could have been easily dismissed. After all, there was no burning bush accompanied by the audible voice of God. There was no flash of light that shone about me. I did not experience any convulsions or any of the spectacular traits associated with being touched by God's Spirit. What I did experience, however, was a profound sense of peace. By peace, I mean an overwhelming sense of assurance, a moment of clarity and the certainty you have when you find the missing piece of a puzzle. It is a peace that passes understanding.

When you have faith, you have peace. When you have peace you have faith. The two are intertwined. Peace is integral to God's character and a powerful ally in making key decisions in your life. There are times when we must take a leap of faith and make decisions based on an optimism that others do not share. In some circles this is called 'crazy' faith. There is nothing crazy in making a leap of faith based on a decision accompanied with a deep sense of peace. Making such a decision, however, *is* crazy if there is no peace - even under the guise of faith. Let me make one thing clear, there is no such thing as blind faith, nor is acting on it reckless! Faith enables one to see far beyond what others can see and is infused with a wisdom capable of bringing unforeseen and unprecedented success. Faith is a verb not a noun; hence the biblical saying - "faith without works is dead." The more you act on faith, the more attuned you will become to spiritual insight.

Get Wisdom

If we are to effectively act on faith, we need wisdom. Wisdom is not just about knowledge, it's about how that knowledge is applied. Seeking wisdom is paramount and more effective than determining what is right or wrong. Rights and wrongs can embroil you in endless debates; but there is little argument when it comes to the question of what is wise and what is foolish. No one wants to be a fool as that is far worse than being wrong.

Perspective

As stated we are both spiritual and physical. We have been designed to thrive on that which motivates, inspires and elevates our thinking. Thus we need to obtain wisdom that will cater for both our spiritual and personal development. This is only achievable when we are willing to see the world and ourselves from a more

◆PREFACE

empowering perspective. Perspective is everything. The view at the foot of a mountain is poles apart from the view at it's peak. The bible is filled with wisdom inviting us to look at things from a different perspective. The poor are told to see themselves as rich. The weak are told to see themselves as strong. We are urged to love our enemies and to turn the other cheek when struck. These things may appear to promote gullibility; but if we could see from the perspective this wisdom stems from, it will make perfect sense to do these things. The biblical account of Elisha's handling of the Syrian army serves to illustrate this point:

THE KING OF SYRIA HAD SENT A WHOLE ARMY TO ARREST ELISHA. THEY CAME BY NIGHT AND SURROUNDED THE CITY WHERE ELISHA AND HIS SERVANT WERE STAYING. WHEN ELISHA'S SERVANT AROSE EARLY AND WENT OUT, HE SAW THE ARMY, SURROUNDING THE CITY WITH HORSES AND CHARIOTS. THE SERVANT SAID TO ELISHA, "ALAS, MY MASTER! WHAT SHALL WE DO?" SO HE ANSWERED, "DO NOT FEAR, FOR THOSE WHO ARE WITH US ARE MORE THAN THOSE WHO ARE WITH THEM." AND ELISHA PRAYED, AND SAID, "LORD, I PRAY, OPEN HIS EYES THAT HE MAY SEE." THEN THE LORD OPENED THE EYES OF THE SERVANT, AND HE LOOKED AND SAW THE HILLS WERE FILLED WITH HORSES AND CHARIOTS OF FIRE ALL AROUND ELISHA (2 KINGS 6:11-17 PARAPHRASED)

There is more working for you than against you. You just need to have your eyes opened.

INTRODUCTION

Pearls of Wisdom serves to opening your eyes to possibilities and realities that will renew your thinking and transform your life. In this book you will find valuable insights and wisdom that will not only cause you to see beyond barriers, but also break the barriers that hinder your success. This book offers you practical insights that address your spiritual and personal development.

Pearls of Wisdom is a collection of lessons in excellence, formulated into four barrier breaking series:

- Self Mastery
- Faith
- The Kingdom
- Personal Power

Each series is designed to equip you with essential life skills and strategies for effective living and success. Using sound biblical success principles and concepts, these 'Pearls' offer cutting edge practical tools on life mastery from a unique perspective.

※INTRODUCTION

Pearls of Wisdom is a result of years of study in the art of excellence. Definitions of excellence abound. However, my definition of excellence is derived from the Apostle Paul's heartfelt plea for us to be transformed by the renewing of our minds (Romans 12:2). The renewing of the mind is not a one time event. It is a continual cycle of learning and improving the quality of our minds. This is the process that enables us to excel in life, as the quality of your life is a reflection of the quality of your mind. Therefore I define excellence as constant advancement by the renewing of our minds. It is my firm belief that biblical principles and Godly wisdom are the key ingredients to truly excel in life.

Lastly, Pearls of Wisdom are lessons learnt from personal experience. Why is personal experience important? Because that is what makes wisdom a pearl. The formation of a pearl begins when a foreign substance slips in between an oyster's mantle and shell, causing irritation. In order to protect itself, the oyster covers the irritant with layers of the same nacre substance that is used to create it's shell. This eventually forms a pearl. Thus, something precious and rare is created from dealing with a painful experience.

My pearls - lessons learned from my triumphs over pain, are also infused within the teachings of this book. Expressing the human experience in the personal journey of faith.

SELF MASTERY

◆SELF MASTERY

EXPOSING HARDNESS OF HEART

THE WORD which came to Jeremiah from the Lord: Arise and go down to the potter's house, and there I will cause you to hear My words. Then I (Jeremiah) went down to the potter's house, and behold, he was working at the wheel. And the vessel that he was making from clay was spoiled in the hand of the potter; so he made it over, reworking it into another vessel as it seemed good to the potter to make it. Jeremiah 18:1-4 (Amplified).

Like clay in the potters hand, God is able to fashion each of us into vessels of honour and purpose. Indeed, great skill and craftsmanship was used to make a vessel that represents the greatness of the potter. Yet with all his skill and greatness, the vessel, while being made, was spoiled in his hand. This does not mean scratched, or dented but completely destroyed. Since God is symbolized by the potter, how is it possible to be destroyed while being made in the skillful and protective hand of God?

For the potter this is not an unusual occurrence. The destruction of a vessel was usually caused by some defect in the walls of the vessel. This defect may be a small stone or a piece of straw in the clay or it maybe nothing more than a small, hard bit of clay that had not yielded to the dampening and kneading process. When the potter's fingers strike the unyielding substance, instead of yielding to the potter's touch, it resists and the entire vessel collapses into an unshapely mass of ugly clay.

The result of having a hard particle in the clay illustrates the consequences of having a hardened or unyielding heart. Proverbs 28:14 says, *"...he who hardens his heart will fall into calamity."* Throughout the bible we see much tragedy resulting from a hardened heart. In the story of Moses we read how Pharaoh's hardened heart brought plague upon plague in Egypt, the destruction of his army and even the death of his firstborn son. Divorce also is a result of a hardened heart (Matthew 19:18). So what is hardness of heart?

The word hard or hardened is a military term which means to strengthen, hold fast, to preserve and to be firm. In ancient Egypt, Pharaohs were worshiped as gods. I believe God hardened Pharaoh's heart (Exodus 7:13) by allowing him to hold fast to the belief that he was a god. Yet at the same time God proved through multiple plagues how ridiculous that belief really was.

The word heart is the Hebrew expression for the mind. Therefore we are actually addressing a state of mind. Hardness of heart is a state of mind that refuses to let go of beliefs that eventually leads to your own demise. From the first few plagues it must have become obvious to Pharaoh that he was no match against the power of the true God. Yet he would not let go of the belief that he was a god. Instead he reached a point where instead of God hardening his heart, he hardened it himself (Exodus 8:15). When you decide to hold fast to certain beliefs your mind subconsciously rejects anything that does not support those beliefs. If you do not believe in God your mind formulates ideas that insulate itself from even the most obvious signs of His existence. This could be one of the reasons why Jesus said *"no man comes to me, except the Father which hath sent me draw him..."* (John 6:44). Past hurts can cause us to formulate and hold fast to certain beliefs that could eventually ruin our lives like the spoilt vessel in the potter's hands.

Exposing hardness of heart is really about examining our underlying beliefs and assumptions. Arguably the most destructive tool in any relationship is assumption. Assumption is defined as belief without proof. Assumption is the lowest form of information, and therefore borderline ignorance. Ignorance (not the devil) is our greatest enemy - My people are destroyed for lack of knowledge (Hosea 3:6). Many of us live by accepted beliefs without proof. We are living in the information age 'where knowledge has increased;' yet we still tend to rely on our assumptions. Acting on assumption instead of questioning them wrecks marriages, maintains poverty, separates friends, fuels racism and hinders progress. The worst thing you can do with an assumption is to past it on to the next generation - in the form of tradition. Religious tradition was the key opponent to Jesus' ministry. He made a point of criticizing the Pharisees for making the Word of God of non effect through their tradition (Mark 7:13). Such is the danger and the power of traditions rooted in assumptions.

Facts vs. Feelings

Much of the conflict that takes place, especially in relationships, can be avoided when we understand the relationship between facts and feelings. Why do we tend to rely so heavily on assumptions? It is because your mind must find a meaning to what you experience. It is the meaning you derive for any given situation that creates your emotional response. Therefore it is a misconception to believe that emotions such as anger, jealousy and fear are all 'natural' reactions. These emotions are created by the 'meaning' you give to the situation. A good meaning triggers pleasurable emotions; a bad meaning triggers painful emotions. You simply cannot feel happy or sad about anything, which has no meaning to you. Hence, emotions are created and controlled by your thoughts and what you perceive to be true. The problem arises when there is a disparity between how you feel about a given situation and the actual facts.

The Map is not the Territory

To give further light on how assumptions are derived, let us look at a map. A map is an artist's impression of a geographical location. The map is merely an illustrative representation it is not reality. The map is not the territory. The map overlooks reams of information in order to present a simplified version of the territory that we can comprehend. Similarly, in order to make sense of the world around you, your mind presents to you its' own artistic impression of what is around you. However, you will never capture all of the complexities of all that is happening around you. Sight is a function of your mind, not your eyes. Your eyes merely serve as a window, but only your mind is capable of defining the images you see through the window. Like a map your mind overlooks a large quantity of information in order to present to you only what is relevant and within your comprehension. You will not see beyond your comprehension. Therefore, your conclusions are self created and may not actually reflect what actually happened. None of us are in the position to see the whole picture in full clarity; we are all looking through a mirror that gives only a dim reflection (1 Corinthians 13:12).

The Things We Believe

How does your mind determine what is represented to you? Well, in order to handle the vast amount of information that you encounter on a daily basis, the human mind (on a subconscious level) only presents to you the things that support your beliefs and values and rejects anything else. For example, if through painful past hurts you have come to the conclusion that all men are cheats or all women are gold diggers, your mind will actively seek for what it would consider 'evidence' to support that claim and overlook the 'evidence' that does not support that belief. We can now see why Jesus said divorce is the result of hardness of heart! When couples refuse to question the validity of their own assumptions and continually make decisions based on those assumptions, it inevitably results in the destruction of the relationship.

Carry out this simple exercise:

Count every ' F ' in the following text:

FINISHED FILES ARE THE RE
SULT OF YEARS OF SCIENTI
FIC STUDY COMBINED WITH
THE EXPERIENCE OF YEARS...

HOW MANY? We'll look at your answer later on.

Distorted Thinking

The meaning we give to any particular event is derived by our own distorted viewpoint and thinking (distortions). Therefore no two people see things in the same way. Even if they were standing together looking at the same thing, each would see something different and draw differing conclusions about what they saw. Distorted thinking does not mean you are warped or twisted. We all look at the world through unique filters, which give us our own perception of reality. These filters are derived by the facets of our personality such as values, beliefs, goals, drivers (the things that motivate you) and principles. Therefore the way you see the world is a reflection of who you are.

The key to exposing hardness of heart is to identify and question our assumptions. In order to do so, we must be aware of our own distortions. These come to light especially when we are upset and experiencing pain. The following are common distortions that influence how we interpret situations:

* Personalization - taking valid comments as personal insults or blaming yourself for something you cannot control.

* All or nothing thinking - seeing events in extreme terms and allowing no room for shades of grey or middle ground.

* Magnification and minimization - exaggerating the negative and minimizing the positive.

- Catastrophizing - imagining or assuming the worst case scenario.

- Over-Generalization - drawing sweeping conclusions based on a single event

Our distortions lead us to jump over a great deal of logic and common sense in order to reach extreme conclusions. These conclusions spawn painful and destructive emotions culminating in a behavioral response that leads to severe consequences.

The Cycle of Emotional Bondage

All painful and emotionally charged situations go through a sequence of events, which if left uninterrupted, spirals into an ongoing cycle of destructive behavior as illustrated in the diagram below.

1. The event or experience

2. Your interpretation of the event (using distorted thinking)

3. The meaning you give to the event (derived from distorted thinking)

4. Emotional response to your meaning

5. behavioral response to your emotion (verbal or physical abuse, self abuse, rash decisions, sexual vice etc.)

6. The consequence of your behavior

7. Leading to another event (retaliation, punishment, divorce, loss of job etc.)

No doubt there are those of you who are totally convinced that your viewpoint and your interpretation of events are totally correct. As far as you are concerned there is no need to question what you believe to be true; it's all there in black and white. Let's look at your answer to our simple brainteaser.

How many F's did you count?
Obviously the answer is 3 right?
Wrong!
Did you see 4?
That's good, but still wrong.

There are actually 6 F's!! Don't believe me? Go back and try to find the F's before you read on.........

Anyone who sees all six the first time is a genius. If you originally saw three, don't despair your normal!

Why didn't you see all 6 F's the first time? It is because your mind did not process the word 'OF". Your mind actually 'skipped' this word, as it was not needed to understand the sentence you were reading. For the majority of us the word 'OF' is unimportant. Incredible, but this is how your mind works. This is not a magic trick or mass hypnosis!

You were so certain there were only 3 F's but now you can see 6. With this in mind look at the conflicts you are experiencing, especially in your marriage or any other relationship. Are the facts really as you see (interpret) them. Or are there things that your mind has overlooked because it was not considered important?

The reverse is also true. There are things we put too much emphasis on that really do not warrant our attention. Simple actions, simple words that should be taken at face value are looked into too deeply, often leading to extreme conclusions. Do you really want people to walk on eggshells around you? You will never achieve intimacy in a relationship where this is the norm.

A Change of Heart

Returning to the illustration of the potter, it is very rare that a potter will rework the same lump of clay that had spoiled in his hand to make another vessel. The normal procedure would be to discard the spoilt clay and use a fresh lump to make another vessel. In order to use the same clay the potter would have to carefully examine and sift through it to find the hard particle responsible for the destruction of the vessel. This act reflects the grace and the mercies of God. Where others are quick to give up on us, He is always willing to give us another chance to change. Hardness of heart need not be permanent; all of us are capable of a change of heart. How can we bring about a change of heart and break the destructive cycle of emotional bondage?

Here are some answers:

Awareness

The first step is to become aware that the condition exists and to know the signs. Hopefully from what you have read thus far, you would have already achieved this. From now on, whenever you see that brainteaser you will always see 6 F's instead of 3. Your mind is now aware and therefore knows not to overlook the F's. In the same manner, through awareness, you will be able to 'catch yourself' making assumptions and forming destructive conclusions without exploring other answers. King Solomon urges us to get wisdom and understanding (Proverbs 4:7). This is critical. It's easy to judge others by their outward behavior. However, all behavior is driven and supported by beliefs. Therefore behavior can only be addressed when we identify and understand the underlying beliefs.

Humility

Hardness of heart is in essence pride. Therefore it is going to take humility to question your assumptions, accept you may have made a mistake and repair the breach in your relationship(s). Humility empowers you to take responsibility. Taking responsibility is not about blame or faultfinding. It is about recognizing your influence in any given situation and taking appropriate action.

Question Your Assumptions

Each of us possesses the unique human endowment of being able to step out of our programming and analyze ourselves. Animals cannot do this - they must follow through on what is instinctive. It is critical that we exercise this ability and question our assumptions even in emotionally charged situations.

Looking back at the diagram, we cannot control (to an extent) the events that happen. However we can control how we respond. The point of control is in stage 2 the place where we give a meaning to what has happened. Instead of jumping to conclusions; the most powerful question we can ask ourselves is - what else could this mean? This question enables us to explore other answers or reasons; after all, there are other viewpoints and methods which are just as credible as your own. This question also enables us to find that critical time needed to respond and not retaliate. Although more difficult, you can also break the cycle at stage 4. This is where you have to quickly deal with the emotions you are feeling before it translates to a behavioral response. This might mean walking away from the situation or doing something bizarre and funny in order to disrupt your natural tendency. This will enable you to back track to stage 2 and think things over. Remember assumptions are beliefs without proof; be cautious about acting upon them. Never make important or critical decisions when you are angry or emotionally charged.

Faith

As previously mentioned, we all view the world from our subjective bias. Each of us distorts reality in accordance with our own disposition. For many of us, fear influences how we see the world. That is why we have a tendency to think the worst. However there is another perspective which in its' purest form allows us to view the world without distortions. This is God's perspective and it's called faith. Faith is the antithesis of fear. Faith is the tool that enables us to master our lives. It brings us into alignment with absolute reality – which ultimately is God. Faith allows us to see possibilities where others cannot. By faith we can focus on our strengths and not our weaknesses, just as God does. Faith is not an assumption (belief without proof). It is the unseen evidence that fuels belief (Hebrews 11:1). By faith we can take control of our circumstances and handle situations in a more productive way.

Wisdom

When you look back at past experiences or relationships, do you ever say to yourself "maybe I could have handled that better?" We're only able to say that now because we have grown in maturity or learned from our mistakes. We all do the best we can with level of maturity, resources and information we have at the time. However we can drastically increase the chances of successfully handling situations now and making better decisions when we make a commitment to our own personal development. In order to get the best out of life we must improve the quality of our mind through wisdom.

Wisdom makes life simple.

IT'S TIME TO GET EXTREME

"If your right eye causes you to sin, pluck it out and cast it from you; for it is more profitable for you that one of your members perish, than for your whole body to be cast into hell. And if your right hand causes you to sin, cut it off and cast it from you; for it is more profitable for you that one of your members perish, than for your whole body to be cast into hell" Matthew 5:29-30 KJV.

If we were to interpret Jesus' words literally we would have to believe that He is advocating the use of self-mutilation as a means of dealing with temptation. However, we would do well to remember Jesus said, *"the words that I have been speaking to you are spirit and life"*

◆SELF MASTERY

> THE HARDEST BATTLE
> IS THE BATTLE AGAINST
> YOUR OWN DESIRES
>
>

(John 6:63). Spirit and life – not flesh and death! Spirit refers to the essence or the heart of the matter. Thus we must learn to grasp the essential principle of what Jesus is saying.

What Jesus is saying in essence is that you may have to resort to extreme actions in order to avoid total ruin and defeat. Especially if *you* are the vehicle for your own destruction. The hardest battle is the battle against your own desires. It is important that you recognize this; not all problems are due to external influences! James 1:13-14 says,

"LET NO MAN SAY WHEN HE IS TEMPTED, I AM TEMPTED OF GOD: FOR GOD CANNOT BE TEMPTED WITH EVIL, NEITHER TEMPTETH HE ANY MAN: BUT EVERY MAN IS TEMPTED, WHEN HE IS DRAWN AWAY OF HIS OWN LUST, AND ENTICED."

You can only be enticed to do something you have a desire to do!

So if you have been prayed for many times and yet you are still caught up in the same cycle of defeat, then it's time to take responsibility for your own actions and stop blaming the devil. Only then will you be able to 'take the bull by the horns' and take charge of your life.

Desire

To clearly understand the problem, let us take an introspective look at ourselves. We are tri-part beings comprised of spirit, soul and body. The spirit is the God-like nature within us that only comes to fruition through the liberating power of Jesus Christ. The spirit can be described as our true nature.

The soul (our personality) is the outcome or reaction of spirit giving life to flesh.

THEN THE LORD GOD FORMED MAN FROM THE DUST OF THE GROUND AND BREATHED INTO HIS NOSTRILS THE BREATH OR SPIRIT OF LIFE, AND MAN BECAME A LIVING BEING [SOUL] (GENESIS 2:7).

The Hebrew word for soul is *'nephesh'* which means 'that which breathes.' It also refers to the 'appetite' or 'desire'. Desire is an integral part of our make up. However, because, of our fallen state our desires are often misplaced. As a matter of fact desire has become synonymous with self-gratification. James 4:1 explains the peril of misplaced desire.

"WHAT LEADS TO STRIFE AND HOW DO CONFLICTS (QUARRELS AND FIGHTINGS) ORIGINATE AMONG YOU? DO THEY NOT ARISE FROM YOUR SENSUAL DESIRES THAT ARE EVER WARRING IN YOUR BODILY MEMBERS? YOU ARE JEALOUS AND COVET [WHAT OTHERS HAVE] AND YOUR DESIRES GO UNFULFILLED; [SO] YOU BECOME MURDERERS. [TO HATE IS TO MURDER AS FAR AS YOUR HEART IS

CONCERNED.] YOU BURN WITH ENVY AND ANGER AND ARE NOT ABLE TO OBTAIN [THE GRATIFICATION, THE CONTENTMENT, AND THE HAPPINESS YOU SEEK], SO YOU FIGHT AND WAR. YOU DO NOT HAVE BECAUSE YOU DO NOT ASK. OR YOU ASK [GOD FOR THEM] AND YET FAIL TO RECEIVE, BECAUSE YOU ASK WITH WRONG MOTIVES. YOUR INTENTION [WHEN YOU GET WHAT YOU DESIRE] TO SPEND IT IN SENSUAL PLEASURES."

Many relationships breakdown through 'unfulfilled desires.' Often times divorce is the devastating results of when expectations meet *reality*. Bad debt is not just a money problem; it is a result of desire and financial ignorance combined. When you act on desires that exceed your financial means, you will inevitably fall into financial difficulty. King Solomon is a tragic example of living a life of self-gratification. His downfall came about due to his immense appetite for foreign women, who turned his heart away from God (1 Kings 11:1-3). However, his greatness came about through his initial desire for something other than himself. When the Lord asked Solomon what he wanted Him to give him, he replied:

".... GIVE YOUR SERVANT AN UNDERSTANDING MIND AND A HEARING HEART TO JUDGE YOUR PEOPLE, THAT I MAY DISCERN BETWEEN GOOD AND BAD" (1 KINGS 3:5-9)

God was pleased at Solomon's request and replied saying:

"BECAUSE YOU HAVE ASKED THIS AND HAVE NOT ASKED FOR LONG LIFE OR FOR RICHES, NOR FOR THE LIVES OF YOUR ENEMIES, BUT HAVE ASKED FOR YOURSELF UNDERSTANDING TO RECOGNIZE WHAT IS JUST AND RIGHT, BEHOLD, I HAVE DONE WHAT YOU HAVE ASKED." (1 KINGS 3:11-12).

As stated, desire is an integral part of our make up. Notice that Solomon desired to be the instrument of blessing towards his people. To do this, he had to become something greater than he already was. This is the type of desire that is pleasing to God - the desire to empower or bless others. Many times we pray for others to be blessed but we are not willing to be the instrument of that blessing. James addresses this in this satirical illustration

"IF A BROTHER OR SISTER IS POORLY CLAD AND LACKS FOOD FOR EACH DAY, AND ONE OF YOU SAYS TO HIM, GOOD-BYE, KEEP YOURSELF WARM AND WELL FED, WITHOUT GIVING HIM THE NECESSITIES FOR THE BODY, WHAT GOOD DOES THAT DO?" (JAMES 2:15-16)

Your Comfort Zone

Deep down we all have this desire to become something great in a way that would impact and improve our community, our nation and our world. As a matter of fact greatness is within you, but unfortunately it is trapped within your flesh. When I say flesh, I am addressing your comfort zone. Staying in your comfort zone can make you lethargic and also gives rise to procrastination. Proverbs 24:33-34 says:

"YET A LITTLE SLEEP, A LITTLE SLUMBER, A LITTLE FOLDING OF THE HANDS TO SLEEP – SO SHALL YOUR POVERTY COME AS A ROBBER AND YOUR WANT AS AN ARMED MAN."

Due to our inclination towards the nature of the flesh, we live our lives according to our comfort zone. We tend not to progress beyond our level of comfort (unless forced to). For example if your financial target is to earn $50K by the end of the year (because that is what you need to be comfortable) and you reach that target in 6 months, you would think logically you would go on to reach $100K by the end of the year. However that may not be the case. If $50K per annum represents your comfort zone, then once you have reached it on a subconscious level you will find every reason not to earn more. You would slow down, go on holidays or even give away or spend any excess. That is because we usually do not progress beyond our level of comfort.

Therefore in order to progress we must raise our level of comfort to new heights! This is only achievable when we learn to curb our appetites and come out of our present comfort zone.

Mastering Your Desires

The proverbs of Solomon were written to help us prudently navigate our way to success in all areas of life. Listen to Solomon's advice on how to conduct yourself before a person of power and influence:

WHEN YOU SIT DOWN TO EAT WITH A RULER, CONSIDER WHO AND WHAT ARE BEFORE YOU; FOR YOU WILL PUT A KNIFE TO YOUR THROAT IF YOU ARE A MAN GIVEN TO DESIRE (PROVERBS 23:2).

BE NOT FORWARD (SELF ASSERTIVE AND BOASTFULLY AMBITIOUS) IN THE PRESENCE OF THE KING, AND STAND OUT IN THE PLACE OF GREAT MEN; FOR BETTER IT IS THAT IT SHOULD BE SAID TO YOU, COME UP HERE, THAN THAT YOU SHOULD BE PUT LOWER IN THE PRESENCE OF THE PRINCE, WHOSE EYES HAVE SEEN YOU (PROVERBS 25:6-7)

In both cases, humility and sobriety over desire is required, and are key qualities for promotion in life. Is it wrong for us to have luxuries or to better ourselves financially? Absolutely not! Not only did God give Solomon the wisdom he asked for, but He also gave him what he did not ask for - riches and honor, more than any king before or after him could equal (1 Kings 3:13). God wants us to master our desires and not become slaves to them. Proverbs 25:4 states; *"take away the dross from the silver, and there shall come forth a vessel for the silversmith."* The dross (waste matter) in our lives represents all the activities we indulge in that do nothing to release our potential or live a truly abundant life. I do not need to draw up a list of these time wasting activities because you already know what they are. Many of them are protected by the excuses you make to condone their existence in your life. God, the great silversmith, wants to mold us into vessels of honor; however, you are going to have to move out of your comfort zone in order for this to happen.

Self-Discipline

Are you willing to make the necessary sacrifices to fulfill your dreams? Are you willing to go that extra mile? Are you willing to push yourself that much more? Are you willing to switch off the TV for a day, a week or even a month? Are you willing to work whilst your friends are out having a good time? Can discipline ever be your friend? How determined are you to save your marriage? Are you willing to accept a different point of view – other than your own? Are you willing to forgive again and again, listen instead of waiting to talk, talk instead of shout? How determined are you to be debt free? Are you willing to sacrifice appearance for achievement? Are you willing to go without luxuries, stop trying to keep up with the Jones' and live within your means, save instead of spend, invest instead of squander, cut up the credit cards and live a modest lifestyle so you can get your finances under control?

Jesus said in Matt 11:12; *"...the Kingdom of Heaven suffers violence and the violent take it by force."* Success is available to all who posses fierce determination and self-discipline to achieve their goals.

The Spirit Led Life

Every one of us has greatness within. It is the key to self-discovery. The road to self-discovery begins when we make the choice to live according to the spirit [disciplined] and not the dictates of the flesh [self gratification with no fulfillment]. There is nothing more rewarding and more fulfilling than to live life according to the Spirit of life in Christ Jesus. This is the only way to connect to your true self, as God sees you, not as people label you.

To aid you on the journey of self-discovery, Jesus said *"I will ask the Father and He will give you another comforter, the Holy Spirit and He will guide you through all truth"* (John 14: 16, 16:3 paraphrase). Here is what is so interesting; comfort is for the flesh, not the spirit. As stated, we do not progress beyond our level of comfort. The Holy Spirit does not just provide comfort; He controls our comfort. As He guides us through all truth, He moves us through one level of comfort to another. There are things that you are not comfortable with now that you were comfortable with *last year*. God causes us

#SELF MASTERY

to advance by taking us to a higher level of comfort. That is why things have to get uncomfortable when we are moving on to the next chapter of our lives. You will never unleash greatness if you are not willing to move out of your present comfort zone. So God raises the standard.

Your spirit-led decisions to move on need to be protected from the allure of your present comfort zone. You may have to burn bridges or set boundaries in order to reach your goal. You may have to develop an all or nothing attitude in key areas of your life. It's going to take extreme measures to get off the treadmill of defeat and despair and onto the road of victory and destiny. This is not an easy task; however, listen to Paul's admonition:

"NO SOLDIER WHEN IN SERVICE GETS ENTANGLED IN THE ENTERPRISES OF [CIVILIAN] LIFE; HIS AIM IS TO SATISFY AND PLEASE THE ONE WHO ENLISTED HIM. AND IF ANYONE ENTERS COMPETITIVE GAMES, HE IS NOT CROWNED UNLESS HE COMPETES LAWFULLY. IT IS THE HARD-WORKING FARMER WHO MUST BE THE FIRST PARTAKER OF THE FRUITS" (2 TIMOTHY 2:3-6)

Life according to the dictates of flesh is like honey - sweet to the taste, but too much is bad for you. Life according to the spirit is like anything else that is good for you – an acquired taste. Once you have acquired a taste for the spirit and see the results, you would be foolish to turn back.

LIVING WITH DIRT

Blessed is the man Who walks not in the counsel of the ungodly, Nor stands in the path of sinners, Nor sits in the seat of the scornful, But his delight is in the law of the Lord, And in His law he meditates day and night. He shall be like a tree Planted by the rivers of water, That brings forth its fruit in its season, Whose leaf also shall not wither; And whatever he does shall prosper. Psalms 1:1-3

In many of the books and teachings I have read on success (especially Christian books), I have found that most authors talk about principles to execute and qualities to develop. Many promote ideals and ignore reality. They focus on strengths rather than weakness.

> WE ARE THE PRODUCT OF THE CHOICES WE MAKE IN OUR ENVIRONMENT
>

Indeed, discipline, integrity, excellence, diligence, focus, goals, planning and faith, to name but a few, are all key ingredients to becoming a high achiever. The bible describes a blessed person as a 'tree' planted by the rivers of water. In other words blessed people live in dirt!

The tallest living tree today (a Redwood) stands at 112 meters, or five stories higher than the Statue of Liberty. It is estimated to be over 1000 years old with a diameter of 3.14m. Imagine standing next to this tree and looking up. You could not help but admire the greatness of this monument of nature. Words such as awesome, magnificent and astonishing would no doubt flood your mind. Compared to this tree you would look like an ant! However in the midst of these accolades the true testimony of this tree, like any other tree, can be found not by looking up at it's height but by looking down at where it's roots lie – in dirt.

The tree tells the story of starting off life in dirt and coming to a place where it was able to push through the dirt and reach for the skies. It is the true success story, from rags to riches, shame to glory. It is the story of how to live in dirt without becoming dirt. By now you have probably made the assumption that dirt is symbolic of adverse circumstances, humble beginnings, deprived living conditions and the like. You would not be far off with that assumption. Many successful people have proved that we are NOT the product of our environment; we are the product of the choices we make IN our environment. In other words you have a choice in how to respond to situations and circumstances no matter how dire they maybe. That is one of the unique God given abilities that separates us from animals.

The question is, 'what is the thought process (beliefs) behind our decisions?' There are those who simply react to their environment (like a thermometer) because they do not believe they have any control over their circumstances. Therefore the prevailing thought is *"do what I have to do to survive"* even at the expense of others. On the other end of the spectrum are those who hold onto ideals that are in no shape or form supported by their present reality. This is the religious end of the spectrum and in particular I am addressing those who adhere to Christian religion rather than Kingdom principles (as taught by Jesus). You may have thought these are two of the same thing, but that is NOT true. Religion is not of God. It is man's own attempt to redeem himself in order to escape a perceived condemnation. It is based on 'assumptions' about what is or is not acceptable to God.

Jesus did not come to establish a religion but a Kingdom; a Kingdom that reconciles a King with his children.

#SELF MASTERY

There are many traits that reveal the differences between the religious and those who are Kingdom minded. The most prominent is where 'the religion' becomes more important than the God it purports to follow. It is not my intention to point the finger or condemn anyone. All of us have been influenced by the teachings of religion and paid the price for it in one form or the other. However because religion is so entrenched within the church, many are unwittingly locked into a cycle of defeat through beliefs and practices they think are Godly.

There is a great deal of ignorance about the relationship between ideals and reality. Reality is the world or the state of things, as they actually exist. An ideal is a conception of smething in its absolute perfection. Religion is solely based on ideals and portrays reality as the enemy, something to be defied or ignored. This dogma is further compounded by a high expectancy of miracles to bail us out of every situation. Anyone not living on this stratosphere of spirituality is considered weak in faith. This has led many to hide their defeats and promote their victories. One sided testimonies based purely on victories devastate the lives of those who try to emulate them because vital truths were missed out or sugar coated in an attempt to 'portray' God in a better light.

In our zeal to prove to unbelievers that salvation does

work we see it as our duty to omit the many defeats we have experienced. To uphold its doctrine of ideals it was religion that invented the concept of God having a plan B, C or D to compensate for the failings in our lives. The truth is that God is a God of reality and not ideals! That is why all who try to live by ideals end up shipwrecked on the rock of reality. Many believe their ideals will cause them to live perfect lives, however, if we are to emulate the perfection of an infinite God then perfection to us must be a process of continual improvement rather than a final state of being.

To clarify, I am not saying it is wrong to have big dreams, vision and aspirations. I would be the first to encourage anyone to do so; but true success can only be realized when we are able to translate our ideals into reality.

Because of this God has inculcated our weaknesses into His plan for our lives. They are actually key elements to our growth and to deny them is to deny the very power of salvation. God is Alpha and Omega – *"declaring the end from the beginning, and from ancient times the things that are not yet done..."* (Isaiah 46:10). Therefore He does not need a plan B for your life. You are still in plan A even though your life is presently in a mess. If we adhere to religious thinking, Jesus would be plan B as a result of Adam (plan A) messing up. The truth is, Jesus was always plan A, because God knew before creation that man would need a savior.

As stated earlier no tree can grow without first being planted in dirt. You were purposely planted in the soil of your environment in order to grow. In that environment you are exposed to many challenging situations that define your strength and exploit your weakness. The essence of what it means to live with dirt is concealed in Jesus' parable of the wheat and the tares.

> THE KINGDOM OF HEAVEN IS LIKE A MAN WHO SOWED GOOD SEED IN HIS FIELD; BUT WHILE MEN SLEPT, HIS ENEMY CAME AND SOWED TARES AMONG THE WHEAT AND WENT HIS WAY. BUT WHEN THE GRAIN HAD SPROUTED AND PRODUCED A CROP, THEN THE TARES ALSO APPEARED. SO THE SERVANTS OF THE OWNER CAME AND SAID TO HIM, 'SIR, DID YOU NOT SOW GOOD SEED IN YOUR FIELD? HOW THEN DOES IT HAVE TARES?' HE SAID TO THEM, 'AN ENEMY HAS DONE THIS.' THE SERVANTS SAID TO HIM, 'DO YOU WANT US THEN TO GO AND GATHER THEM UP?' BUT HE SAID, 'NO, LEST WHILE YOU GATHER UP THE TARES YOU ALSO UPROOT THE WHEAT WITH THEM. LET BOTH GROW TOGETHER UNTIL THE HARVEST, AND AT THE TIME OF HARVEST I WILL SAY TO THE REAPERS, "FIRST GATHER TOGETHER THE TARES AND BIND THEM IN BUNDLES TO BURN THEM, BUT GATHER THE WHEAT INTO MY BARN" (MATTHEW 13:25-30)

In Jesus' interpretation of this parable he says, *"the good seed are the children of the Kingdom and the tares are the children of the wicked one."* Theologians would normally define these as two types of people coexisting together, although there is some debate into the true identity of these people. However, I invite you to look at this parable from a different perspective, where the good seed represent our strengths and the tares represent our weaknesses (failings). Our strengths are from God and our weaknesses are from the enemy. Both coexist together in such a way that you cannot extract one without destroying the other.

In the early stages of growth, the wheat and the tares are almost indistinguishable. It is only when the wheat bears fruit that you can tell them apart. In like manner, your weakness becomes more of an issue as you grow and bear fruit. Even spiritual growth will not eradicate your weaknesses. It is an armour indeed, but not without chinks.

Therefore it is imperative that you do not let your weaknesses serve as an excuse to stop growing. Do not let guilt abort your mission.

"IF OUR HEARTS CONDEMN US, GOD IS GREATER THAN OUR HEARTS" (1 JOHN 3:20)

God's focus is on your strengths, not your weakness. As a matter of fact His strength is made perfect in weakness (2 Corinthians 12:9). The best listeners in the world are blind people! They hear things we tend to overlook. In like manner our weaknesses serve to develop our strengths and helps us to deal with life's 'grey' areas rather than seeing everything in black and white.

Do not try to live up to the ideals of others. Deal with the reality of your situation for that is where God is. Learn how to translate the high standards of God's Word into your reality, just as Esther, Joseph, Nehemiah and Daniel did. The bible illustrates how these 4 successfully lived and found favor in an ungodly environment without compromising their faith.

Keep on going despite the challenges and the defeats. You can triumph with weakness! That being said, there is a time (Harvest), when the wheat is separated from the tares through a process of sifting and threshing. In like manner when we reach a place of maturity we experience a time of threshing and sifting in order to perfect our strengths and diminish our weaknesses. Don't try to skip this necessary process for it will serve to elevate you.

In closing, no matter how high a tree grows, it is still in contact with dirt. You are only as effective in life as your ability to relate to the reality of others. Hebrews 4:15 states;

"for we have not an high priest which cannot be touched with the feeling of our infirmities; but was in all points tempted like as we are, yet without sin."

PASSION KILLERS

The effective, fervent prayer of a righteous man avails much. Elijah was a man with a nature like ours, and he prayed earnestly that it would not rain; and it did not rain on the land for three years and six months. And he prayed again, and the heaven gave rain, and the earth produced its fruit. James 5:16-18.

Arguably the most dramatic display of God's power in the bible was seen through the prophet Elijah. At his request fire came down from heaven, a child was brought back to life, rain ceased for three and a half years and much more besides. His departure from this life was just

> THE HARDEST BATTLE IS THE BATTLE AGAINST YOUR OWN DESIRES
>

as spectacular when he was carried up to heaven in a whirlwind proceeded by a chariot and horses of fire. It is interesting that the bible describes this mighty prophet as a man subject to like passions as we are. A man subject to the same emotional ups and downs that is inherent in human nature. Like David, Daniel, Samson and many others in the bible, passion was the key to the great anointing on his life.

"I HAVE BEEN VERY JEALOUS FOR THE LORD GOD OF HOSTS, BECAUSE THE ISRAELITES HAVE FORSAKEN YOUR COVENANT, THROWN DOWN YOUR ALTARS AND SLAIN YOUR PROPHETS WITH THE SWORD..." (1 KINGS 19:14)

The word jealous in this context means to burn with zeal and passion. Nothing else triggers the move of God in our lives like passion. It is impossible to love God with all our heart, soul and might without passion. Passion energizes our prayers and our faith.

The Oxford dictionary defines passion as strong and barely controllable emotions. Jeremiah described it as 'burning fire shut up in his bones' when he tried to stop himself from preaching God's Word (Jeremiah 20:9).

It was passion (zeal) that drove Jesus to physically attack the money changers and drive them out of the temple (John 2:15-17). As Elijah's protégé, Elisha saw the connection between his passion and the power that was made available to him. Hence when it was time for him to succeed Elijah, his one request was to have a double portion of Elijah's spirit (2 Kings 2:9). Elisha wanted twice the intensity of Elijah's passion for God. When he received it the impact was such that long after he had died his bones were able to bring a man back to life (2 Kings 13:21).

Passion is an overwhelming and consuming desire that has the ability to push pass all our fears and inhibitions with an unstoppable urge to achieve our goals. Often times the word desire is met with unease, especially in religious circles. It conjures up thoughts of lust, greed and covetousness. However, life without desire and the fulfillment of it is meaningless.

The human soul is the embodiment of desire. We see this in the Hebrew word for soul, *'nephesh'*, which makes reference to the will, desire and appetite of man. We are all people subject to desires and emotions. Emotions are the basis of the human experience. Everyday of our lives are spent on handling how we express our desires and emotions. All that is good or bad in our lives and in this world centers around desire and emotions.

Passion's Killer

All emotions are in essence the impulse to act. Nothing happens without emotion. Passion, the strongest of all human emotion, intensifies our actions and validates our commitment to a cause. There is, however, another type of emotion that has the ability to douse the flames of passion if left unchecked. The bible calls it slothfulness or laziness in modern terminology. Laziness is the antithesis of emotion in that it is the impulse for inaction. Laziness is to passion what fear is to faith. Laziness is a passion killer! The bible has much to say about laziness, none of it complimentary and often expressed with satirical disdain:

THE SLUGGARD BURIES HIS HAND IN THE DISH, AND WILL NOT SO MUCH AS BRING IT TO HIS MOUTH AGAIN - PROVERBS 19:24

THE SLUGGARD SAYS, "THERE IS A LION OUTSIDE, I SHALL BE SLAIN IN THE STREETS" - PROVERBS 22:13

AS THE DOOR TURNS ON ITS HINGE, SO DOES THE LAZY MAN ON HIS BED - PROVERBS 26:14

The bible asserts, *"people are destroyed through a lack of knowledge"* (Hosea 4:6). Added to this I would say, "People are destroyed through a lack of *action*." There are people who have attended a multitude of conferences, seminars and courses, yet with all the knowledge they have heard, there is still no significant progress to their lives. This is because many hear but few act on what they have heard. Wisdom brings success (Ecclesiastes 10:10). Many seek wisdom but fail to realize that wisdom is the application of knowledge. Faith without works is truly dead (James 2:17). A preacher can feed your faith; however, it's going to take action on your part to make it work. The failure to act ultimately leads to the demise of all that you desire to achieve in life.

On a surface level we would describe a lazy person as someone who lacks any desire to work or make an effort. Laziness, however, comes in different forms and is not just a matter of having a poor work ethic. As a matter of fact you can work all day and still suffer from laziness.

THE WAY OF THE SLOTHFUL MAN IS AS A HEDGE OF THORNS, BUT THE WAY OF THE RIGHTEOUS IS MADE PLAIN" (PROVERBS 15:19).

Like barbed wire, a hedge of thorns is a type of barrier used to keep out intruders. An encounter with this barrier usually results in pain. The hedge of thorns as depicted in Proverbs 15:19 represents a mental barrier. This barrier comes to light when particular activities have a strong association with pain. It is important to note that this barrier is formed by the perception of pain, not the presence of it.

Thus on a deeper level, laziness is not just a matter of 'I can't be bothered' but a reaction to perceived pain. It is the impulse that is triggered when a particular activity conjures up painful thoughts.

'THE DESIRE OF THE SLOTHFUL MAN KILLS HIM, FOR HIS HANDS REFUSE TO LABOR....' (PROVERBS 21:25)

The plight of those afflicted with this mental barrier is that they have dreams and ambitions, but lack the passion or the enthusiasm to do the work. This, indeed, can be a source of great frustration. In order to unlock the shackles of laziness we must delve deeper to the core of laziness. Although pain is often seen as a barrier, pain is just as strong a motivator as pleasure. For example: in many instances the pain of being overweight can be the motivating factor for someone going to the gym and changing their diet, rather than the pleasure of being toned and healthy. When you are passionate about something, you are willing to endure pain in order to achieve your goal(s). Therefore perceived pain is not the true source of laziness, it is only a by-product.

The conclusion to Proverbs 21:25 reads:

'HE COVETS GREEDILY ALL DAY LONG, BUT THE RIGHTEOUS GIVES AND DOES NOT WITHHOLD'

Notice how the bible associates greed and covetousness with laziness. Greed and covetousness are the hallmarks of someone who always seeks immediate gratification.

This is what lies at the core of laziness. Thus laziness is selfishness by nature. The reluctance to work relates to the lack of gratification more than the presence of pain. This is why someone can be very active in certain areas of their life but inactive (lazy) in others. They find immediate gratification in the activities they do and shy away from activities where the benefits don't come as quick as they would like. For example there are those who can do a two hour intense work out in the gym but struggle to pray for five minutes. The need for immediate gratification can lead to an inability to successfully manage the ups and downs of life. It also fosters a 'something for nothing' mentality. When life is reluctant to meet the demand for immediate gratification, those who have this expectation often resort to extreme measures to get what they want.

A lifestyle centered around immediate gratification is a lying vanity. Like drugs, there is never any real fulfillment. It just creates a void of emptiness in your life. This void is likened to *chronic* boredom. Boredom is the hub for deviancy. A rather precarious survey was carried out on people who had lost everything they had (including their dignity) due to their addiction to crack cocaine. These were people who would resort to absolutely anything to feed their drug addiction. The question was asked about what got them on drugs in the first place. There were various answers such as being introduced to it by friends and peer pressure; but the most common answer was *sheer boredom*. Boredom and laziness is a lethal cocktail with devastating results. They have the ability to keep you locked in a never-ending cycle of frustration, vice and pitiful excuses for not being able to succeed. Laziness and boredom are passion killers. A life without passion is mere existence.

Bring back the Passion

God abhors laziness and despite the negative press, He certainly is not boring. As a matter of fact the word 'enthusiasm' originates from the Greek term 'possessed by a god.' You cannot serve God without passion! We were made to be passionate about something. When Goliath defied the armies of Israel, stirred by passion David (a man described as having the heart of God) cried *"is there not a cause?"* (1Samuel 17:29). Is there a cause you are passionate about? What is stopping you from fighting for that cause? Are you waiting for others to bring about the change you desire to see? Have you allowed circumstances to take the wind out your sail? It is never too late to ignite the passion you once had and start to really live again. Here are some ways to igniting the flames of passion in your life:

Embrace the Benefits of Delayed Gratification

There are an array of hidden benefits that come with practicing delayed gratification. Food tastes that much sweeter when you wait for it. Your appreciation of what you gain in life is far greater when you have diligently worked for it. Patience indeed has its rewards and more pleasure can be gained from delayed gratification as opposed to immediate. Instant gratification cheapens our experience of life and robs us of the blessings that patience brings. Delayed gratification brings a beauty to life, which cannot be imitated.

The truth of the matter is, some things must precede other things. This is a hard lesson for those who are always looking for quick fix solutions. David showed his understanding of this when he spared the life of Saul his enemy. Although David had been anointed King of Israel he chose not to usurp the authority of Saul and instead waited on God's timing (1 Samuel 24). God is a god of process and that process consists of times and seasons. A person of quality is one who takes the time to learn the lessons that process teaches, instead of trying to skip it.

Delayed gratification builds momentum. The more you practice it, the more results you see. The more results you see, the more inspired and enthused you become. The more enthused you become the more motivated you become, which in turn leads to more action and greater results.

Become Action Oriented

Wisdom and knowledge serve as instructions; they are not meant to just tickle your ears. Instructions are pointless unless they are acted upon. Make a decisive commitment to becoming action orientated. It's going to take discipline, but it is the most effective tool for getting out of the rut of laziness and complacency. To quote Zig Ziglar:

"DISCIPLINE YOURSELF TO DO THE THINGS THAT YOU NEED TO DO WHEN YOU NEED TO DO THEM, AND THE DAY WILL COME WHEN YOU WILL BE ABLE TO DO THE THINGS YOU WANT TO DO WHEN YOU WANT TO DO THEM!"

Connect with Your Purpose

We were all made for a purpose. Each of us has a place in life's great jigsaw puzzle. Nothing makes you feel more alive than fulfilling your God-given purpose. God made each of us unique, and embedded in our uniqueness lies solutions for alleviating the pain and suffering of others in any capacity. Can one person make a difference? The answer is yes! The bible is full of individuals whom God used to impact their community, their nation and their world. The history books are full of ordinary people who made an extraordinary difference to the world. Passion is the driving force for making positive and lasting change. Finding your passion connects you to your purpose.

Sometimes finding your passion means finding your pain first. Indeed, passion is born from a first hand experience of what needs to be changed. Mahatma Ghandi and Martin Luther King, Jr's passion for civil rights was born out of the pain of racial discrimination and injustice. Maya Angelou endured poverty, abusive relationships and violence before becoming one of America's most prominent writers and artists. You cannot afford to sit by the sidelines the rest of your life and complain about the irritations of life. Turn your complaints into solutions and start to do something about the problems that are close to your heart.

Get Closer to the Source

When God created the earth, He designed everything to be sustained by their particular source. For example, the earth is the source and sustainer of animals and vegetation. The Heavens are the source and sustainer of the stars and the planets and the waters sustain the fish and creatures of the sea. In each case God spoke to the source in order to bring forth its particular fruit. When it came to the business of creating man God spoke to Himself saying, *"Let Us make man in Our own image, after Our likeness..."* (Genesis 1:26) indicating that He was to be the source and sustainer of man. Just as trees need to remain planted in soil in order to function, we too need to be connected to God in order to function according to His design. When you get closer to the source you will be infected by His overwhelming passion for the well being of mankind.

Although we are far from the majestic beings He created us to be, the virtues we call humanity are all but the shattered fragments of His character that remain within us. We often look to the man or woman of our dreams to complete us, but it is only through reconciliation with God our Father, through Christ, that we can become whole again. When we learn to push pass the veil of religion (which only serves to distort our perception of God) not only will we see a true reflection of God but a true reflection of ourselves.

FAITH

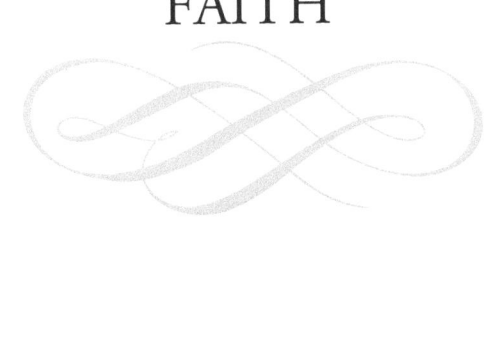

✦FAITH

PERCEPTION

The eye is the lamp of the body. So if your eye is sound, your entire body will be full of light. But if your eye is unsound, your whole body will be full of darkness. If then the very light in you is darkened, how dense is that darkness!
Matthew 6:22-23.

Your perception of the events that occur in your life will determine how you feel and react to them. For example if an event occurs that could be deemed as negative or challenging, one person may see great opportunity, while another will view the same thing as

> FAITH SEES DOORS
> WHERE OTHERS
> SEE WALLS

a great loss. Our emotions and emotional response all stem from the way we 'view' things. It is from our perspective that we interpret and derive a 'meaning' to an event. For example if you are standing at the foot of a mountain, that mountain may look intimidating, challenging or even impossible to overcome. On the other hand, if you are soaring high above the mountain all you will see is a bump on the landscape. Same mountain, different perspective.

We all tend to distort reality in one way or the other by the way we perceive the world. Distorted thinking does not mean that you are a warped or twisted. Our values, beliefs and experiences determine the way we see the world and no two people see it the same. Compare someone with 20/20 vision and another who is short sighted. The person with 20/20 vision is able to see further with clarity and detail. With the short sighted person, it is not that he cannot see things at a distance, but what he sees is fuzzy and blurred, with no clarity or definition. Therefore he is not able to clearly discern what he is looking at, only guess.

Many of us live our lives through guesswork or assumption. Through our short – sightedness we may assume that at a distance a tall monster with a big green head and long brown legs is in front of us, only to find when we get closer, that it is only *a tree*. This may be an absurd example but I hope you see my point. The assumption that a monster is in the way may stop us from moving forward. That monster could be adult education, setting up a business, attending interviews and a host of other perceived problems. Unfortunately, many of us act upon negative assumptions that hinder our progress or cause us to go off track and pass over opportunities.

Almost all of these negative assumptions stem from fear. Fear distorts the way we think and causes us to focus on our problems rather than solutions. If we go back to the temptation in the garden of Eden, the serpent convinced Eve that it would be to her advantage to eat the fruit from the tree of the knowledge of good and evil, so she could be like God, knowing the difference between good and evil. What she and Adam did not count on was the fear factor that was also unleashed into their lives. We know fear was present because they hid from the presence of God. It is because of fear that we have a tendency to expect a negative outcome when it could just as easily be positive.

Imagine if the concept of evil did not exist in your mind. As far as you were concerned, nothing could go wrong. What would that do for your confidence, your attitude and your self-esteem? How would that affect your performance in whatever you were doing? Your confidence would go through the roof, you would possess a totally positive mental attitude and an ultra high esteem. You would be totally fearless and absolutely unstoppable in your performance and the achievement of goals. What I just described may seem like a pipe dream in such a turbulent world, but it is possible when we live by faith. Faith enables us to see things from God's perspective, not man's. Jesus said, *"with men this is impossible; but with God all things are possible"* (Matthew 19:26).

With our short sightedness and distorted thinking we will always see impossibilities. But the reality is, God has made all things possible. Everything can be achieved by faith. Faith sees doors where others see walls. Faith sees success where others see failure. With faith nothing can go wrong. You may be thinking, "that's not realistic, things go wrong all the time," but that depends on how you define wrong. Things may not go as you expect, but did it really go wrong? There are many successful people who attribute the failures in their lives to their success. The truth is we are surrounded with opportunities all the time. Faith enables us to recognize opportunities others can't see. Faith elevates our thinking to a heavenly perspective where mountains are just bumps on the landscape.

So what is faith? As previously stated, fear distorts the

way we think so that we do not see things as they really are. Faith is the very opposite of fear. Faith gives us an undistorted view of all that is possible in life. Faith gives us 20/20 vision with the ability to see long range with clarity. This is because faith always comes with vision, for nothing is achieved without first having a vision of the finished product. All that is tangible was once intangible. Vision is the intangible evidence of what will be tangible.

How are we able to see the vision? Through imagination! God did not give you the ability to imagine just so you could fantasize. In the biblical account of the tower of Babel (Genesis 11:1-9), the inhabitants of the earth planned to build a tower that would reach heaven. The bible says, *"the Lord came down to see the city and the tower, which the sons of men had built"* (past tense). The strange thing is that the work had not been completed (and was probably at the beginning stages). We know this because when the Lord had confounded their language, causing them to scatter, Genesis 11:8 states; *"...and they gave up building the city."*

So, where was the completed city and tower that the Lord saw? It existed in the minds and imagination of the sons of men. Obviously, the Lord took this very seriously, otherwise he would not of taken such drastic steps to prevent them from building it. Listen to what God says of the sons of men:

✦FAITH

"...NOTHING THEY HAVE IMAGINED THEY CAN DO WILL BE IMPOSSIBLE FOR THEM" (GENESIS 11:6)

Imagination is key to manifestation.

Faith is activated and depends on the level of confidence you have in what you hope for (Hebrews 11:1). However, what you hope for must be consistent with the promises of God. Therefore to the degree of trust you have in the promises of God, is the degree it will work for you. Many of us have asked the question, 'will this happen for me?' The answer to this question can be found in 2 Corinthians 1:20 *"for as many as are the promises of God, they all find their Yes in Him. For this reason we also utter the Amen (so be it) to God through Him to the glory of God."* There's your answer, He says, "yes" we say, "so be it".

There are great success technicians that teach on the principles of success. Faith encompasses and transcends all of the principles taught. Romans 1:17 states; *"for therein is the righteousness of God revealed from faith to faith: as it is written, The just shall live by faith."* The righteousness of God is His standard of living. God's standards are high and He expects us to live at that level, morally, spiritually, financially, emotionally and physically. This can only be achieved through a faith-based lifestyle. A lifestyle void of faith is simply substandard.

OVERCOMING THE FEAR OF FAILURE

But God faced him directly: "Go in this strength that is yours. Save Israel from Midian. Haven't I just sent you?" Gideon said to him, "Me, my master? How and with what could I ever save Israel? Look at me. My clan's the weakest in Manasseh and I'm the runt of the litter." Judges 6:14-15 (The Message)

Our perception of failure is one of the (if not the only) deciding factors as to whether we will have success or not. The difference between average people and achieving people is their attitude and response to failure. Nothing else has the same kind of impact on people's ability

✦FAITH

FAILURE IS IN THE EYE OF THE BEHOLDER

to achieve whatever their heart desires. If you want to be an achiever in life then you need to redefine your perception of success and failure. For many, failure has been a reason to give up on their dreams, ambitions or even life. To quote General Douglas McArthur:

"AGE WRINKLES THE BODY. QUITTING WRINKLES THE SOUL."

WE NEED JUST AS MUCH TRAINING FOR FAILURE AS WE DO FOR SUCCESS. FAILURE IS FAR MORE COMMON THAN SUCCESS (J. WALLACE HAMILTON).

Please note: I am not advocating negative thinking but a more panoramic viewpoint. There are many who live with the pain and disappointment of past failure(s), which prevents them from moving on in life. If we look deeper at what is really holding them back, we will find fear at the root of the problem. Fear has the power to paralyze our goals. Ironically its' power lies only in its' ability to deceive us.

The most successful of fears' arsenal of deception is the fear of failure. The fear of failure will stop you from setting up a business, writing that book, going to college again, public speaking, being a responsible parent; the list is inexhaustible. One man's dream can improve the lives of millions. One man's dream can change the world for the better. Tragically, the fear of failure has sent many dreams to an early grave.

There are many who get caught in the cycle of fear, when they fail to overcome past failings or prior negative experiences. Does this happen to you?

* When you get the opportunity to do something you failed at in the past, fear strikes your heart.

* Fear paralyzes you into inaction, therefore you pass up the opportunity.

* Because you have not tried to do it again you gain no experience.

* Your inexperience therefore breeds insecurities.

* This in turn brings you back to fear again and the cycle continues each time reinforcing your excuse for not achieving your goals.

If this is your experience, then it's time to break out of the cycle of fear!

Many people try to eliminate fear before they can act, but this is not always possible. The stage of inaction is the most effective place to break the cycle of fear.

❋FAITH

When you can take action despite feeling fearful, you have broken the cycle of fear. Whenever you want to achieve something of significance, fear counteracts with plausible reasons why it is not possible or worth-while. The bible gives an account where the children of Israel were at the edge of Canaan, the Promise land. God ordered Moses to send out spies on a reconnaissance mission. Moses sent out a team of 12 leaders and when they returned they gave a split verdict. This was the report from 10 of the 12:

"WE ARE NOT ABLE TO GO UP AGAINST THE PEOPLE, FOR THEY ARE STRONGER THAN WE." AND THEY GAVE THE CHILDREN OF ISRAEL A BAD REPORT OF THE LAND WHICH THEY HAD SPIED OUT, SAYING, "THE LAND THROUGH WHICH WE HAVE GONE AS SPIES IS A LAND THAT DEVOURS ITS INHABITANTS, AND ALL THE PEOPLE WHOM WE SAW IN IT ARE MEN OF GREAT STATURE. THERE WE SAW THE GIANTS (THE DESCENDANTS OF ANAK CAME FROM THE GIANTS); AND WE WERE LIKE GRASSHOPPERS IN OUR OWN SIGHT, AND SO WE WERE IN THEIR SIGHT" (NUMBERS 13:31-33)

Compare their report to the other two:

THEN CALEB QUIETED THE PEOPLE BEFORE MOSES, AND SAID, "LET US GO UP AT ONCE AND TAKE POSSESSION, FOR WE ARE WELL ABLE TO OVERCOME IT" (NUMBERS 13:30)

The question you must ask yourself is - "who's report should you believe?" The voice of the majority or the minority report? The majority saw themselves as grasshoppers. Not only that, they also thought the inhabitants of the land would see them as grasshoppers. That is how the fear of failure works. First you see yourself in a less than significant position in comparison to others. Then you think others see you that way too.

History shows that the minority report was the better report. The reconnaissance mission was never intended to ascertain whether they should take the land or not. After all, taking the land was their whole purpose. Although the voice of fear is loud, sometimes deafening, it is the still small voice of faith (the minority report) that you must listen to. Faith will always support your purpose and guide you through every obstacle.

Notice Caleb said *"let us go up at once..."* He probably saw the poisonous fumes of procrastination creeping into the camp. Procrastination fosters fear, steals time, stops productivity and stifles potential. Procrastination is the fertilizer that makes difficulties grow. The children of Israel ended up circling the desert for forty years because of it; at the very brink of achieving their goal. Don't let this happen to you! Develop a DO IT NOW attitude before procrastination robs you of your destiny. In life the question is not 'if' you will have challenges, but 'how' you overcome challenges?

"A righteous man falls seven times and rises again." (Proverbs 24:16)

✦FAITH

Life is not a 100m dash, it's a steeplechase; an endurance race with many ditches and hurdles. It is the challenges in life that propels you. Competition can be a threat to many businesses but a business without competition has no incentive to improve. The very thing that opposes you also *propels you.*

You have the ability to overcome any challenge, mistake or misfortune, when you change your mindset about failure and learn to fail successfully. Yes, it is possible to have *successful failures*. Although the words success and failure seem to be poles apart by definition, if we learn how to marry the two we create a winning combination.

Failing successfully is the ability to turn mistakes into stepping stones for success. Is there a failing or mistake in your past that is preventing you from carrying out the desire in your heart? It may be in the area of business, ministry or relationships. If you cannot look beyond past failings then you're at a full stop. No matter how big or painful the fall, you can always rise from the ashes if you learn to convert failings into tools for success.

How to Fail Successfully

We can learn to fail successfully by adopting a more radical approach to failure:

Failure is your Friend and Mentor
Failure is not your enemy, but a friend who will provide lessons in life in order to equip you. You must learn from the lessons. If you don't the lessons are repeated and often get harder and are more painful. You'll know you've learned a lesson when your actions have changed.

Failure is in the Eye of the Beholder
What determines whether you have failed or not? Is it the size of the problem or the amount of criticism you receive? Don't let failure define you. Only you can decide if you have failed or not. Failure is subjective. One man's failure is another man's success. You only fail when you tell yourself you have failed. We may have failings but that does not make us failures. Remember it's not over until you say it's over!

Failure is Not a Stigma
Don't be afraid to let others know that you have messed up; we all have that in common. Embrace failure as a friend and don't let the negative opinions of others hold you back.

Failure is Not Final
Don't throw the baby out with the bath water just because of a mistake. Keep things in perspective by looking at the bigger picture. Many of life's failures are people who did not realize how close they were to

success when they gave up - Thomas Edison.

Reverse Paranoia

Learn how to turn negative experiences into positive ones by developing a reverse paranoia attitude. That is, instead of believing that everyone is working towards your demise, believe that 'everything' is working towards your good:

AND WE KNOW THAT ALL THINGS WORK TOGETHER FOR GOOD TO THOSE WHO LOVE GOD, TO THOSE WHO ARE THE CALLED ACCORDING TO HIS PURPOSE (ROMANS 8:28)

When you frame your view of the world with this kind of thinking you will be unstoppable when it comes to achieving your goals.

MANIFSTING THE PROMISE

God is not unjust; he will not forget your work and the love you have shown him as you have helped his people and continue to help them. We want each of you to show this same diligence to the very end, in order to make your hope sure. We do not want you to become lazy, but to imitate those who through faith and patience inherit what has been promised. Hebrews 6:10-12 NIV.

God's will and desire for your life comes in the form of a promise. This promise is packaged as a *seed* which He plants in the hearts of each and every one of us. Evidence of this seed is the vision and calling that is tugging on your heart to achieve something great. It

◆FAITH

Your heart is the control centre of your world

is the one thing that we must achieve before we die. It is the thing that would make all the difference to our lives and the lives of others and bring us to a place of total fulfillment. In the opening text, Paul makes an important distinction between our labor of love in ministering to the needs of others and realizing the promises of God for our lives. The willingness to serve is the prerequisite to becoming a leader in your own right. It is important to submit under the leadership of others and aid in realizing their vision. However there comes a time when you must answer the call of your own vision and pursue it with all diligence. Our prime responsibility is to discover, develop and deploy the gift that God has given to us. We do not have the right to just sit on our gift (Matthew 25:24-30).

So how do we manifest the promise of God for our lives? According to Paul it is through faith and patience. Let us look at these two aspects in more detail:

The Dynamics of Faith

Arguably the most concise illustration Jesus gave on the dynamics of faith is the parable of the sower. In this parable the word of the Kingdom (represented by seeds) is sowed and scattered across four types of surface conditions: the wayside, stony or shallow ground, thorns and good soil. These surfaces represented different types of heart conditions. It is only in the good soil that the seed is able to take root and bring forth fruit. What we are seeing here is the synergy that takes place between mind (heart) and spirit. Jesus said, *"the words that I speak unto you are spirit and life"* (John 6:63). Words are more than a form of communication, they are *spiritual containers*. Spirit is in essence life; therefore words (especially God's Word) are full of life.

Proverbs 4:23 instructs us to, 'keep and guard our hearts with all diligence for out of it flows the issues of life.' It is through the heart (mind) where manifestation of God's Word for our lives takes place. All the issues of our lives stem from and are determined by the condition of our heart.

Your heart is the control center of your world. Your heart is the incubator of God's Word. Spirit and mind are designed to work together, not in isolation. That is why James declares, *"faith without works is dead"* (James 2:20). There must always be a natural correlation to spiritual pursuits. To put it another way, your actions must be congruent with your faith. That is why 'belief' is the key element of faith, because all of your actions stem from what you believe.

❋FAITH

That being the case, your 'psychology' is also critical to your faith as it is fundamental to your beliefs. Your psychology (to put it simply) is the combination of your rules, values and attitude to any given situation. When your psychology is in agreement with God's Word there is nothing you will not be able to achieve. That is why the most effective people on the planet are those who are able to combine theology (spiritual) with psychology (natural).

This model for success can be found in the work of Dr. Norman Vincent Peale, an ordained minister and pastor who blended psychotherapy with theology. A prolific writer, his highly acclaimed book 'The Power of Positive Thinking' (a phenomenal best-seller written over 50 years ago) still impacts millions today. Over the past generation the church has experienced unprecedented growth due to the shift in preaching psychology as well as theology.

Taking all this into account, the dynamics of faith boils down to taking a seed (in the form of a Word from God that addresses our need) and planting it in our hearts where it will take root and grow until we see the manifestation. The soil of your heart must contain nutrients conducive to the growth of that seed. These nutrients come in the form of corresponding beliefs, knowledge, principles and values; all of the things that make up your psychology. To ensure the right nutrients are present you must water your heart with God's Word and information conducive with what you want to manifest in your life.

The Need for Patience

The dynamics of faith is likened to the process of germination. Germination is the growth of an embryonic plant contained within a seed. The things that God has promised for your life will come as a result of germination in your heart. Germination is dependent on both internal and external conditions. Therefore in order for germination to take place the right environment must be present. This is why germination does not happen immediately. It only happens after a period of dormancy. This period is known as seed dormancy. The length of dormancy is dependent upon the nature of the seed and the environment it requires. Different variety of seeds require distinctive variables for successful germination. Some seeds germinate in cold soil, whilst most germinate in the warmth. Some seed require light and others require darkness. It all depends on the individual seed and its nature.

In like manner your time of manifestation is dependent on the nature of your purpose. The conditions that worked for someone else may not necessarily work for you. Depending on the nature of your purpose you may have to go through a period of darkness while others need light. Like a cactus, you may flourish in hostile conditions where others cannot. Places and activities that are questionable to others may be totally necessary for you. When your environment becomes conducive to the character of your seed, it induces germination. This is called the dormancy release factor. The dormancy release factor removes all the 'barriers' that prevents germination.

As previously mentioned, the seed (Word), in Jesus' parable of the sower, only flourished in good soil. It is interesting to note that the Greek word used for good is *kalos* which primarily means 'beautiful'. It has nothing to do with benevolence. Beauty is a relative term (beauty is in the eye of the beholder); what is beautiful to one, may be repulsive to another. Therefore only the seed can determine the beauty of the soil.

Ecclesiastes 3:11 says that God makes everything beautiful in His time. Never think God's delays are His denials. He is working on your heart and your environment to bring you to your place and time of beauty. It is in your time of beauty that you will see the manifestation of God's promise. This takes time and patience. The barriers that are before you, the things that are hindering your success may have more to do with your environment than your behavior. What you need is the dormancy release factor to break down the barriers. Consider the environment you are in right now. This may be your job, your social setting or even the country you live in. These factors and many more can stifle your growth. Your place of beauty may be in your own business rather than a job. Your place of beauty may be in another country. Your place of beauty maybe with someone or without. Maybe you should be an actress instead of an accountant, a musician instead of a lawyer. Remember it is the nature of your seed that determines the beauty of the soil and the environment; not the opinion of others.

❖FAITH

STRONG FAITH

We who are strong in our convictions and of robust faith ought to bear with the failings and the frailties and the tender scruples of the weak and not to please ourselves. Romans 15:1

In tackling the subject of strong faith, I believe it is important to first address the underlying message that Paul is communicating in Romans 14. That message is love expressing itself in sensitivity for each other's convictions. Believers have differing beliefs regarding what is acceptable and unacceptable before God. There are contrasting views regarding dress code, music, days of worship, type of worship, food, the amount of money one should have or should not have, and a host of other issues concerning moral conduct. It is important for us to be mindful of these issues and to realize that these differing viewpoints are all for the purpose of honoring the Lord according to our values and the level of our understanding (Romans 14:6).

AS FOR THE MAN WHO IS A WEAK BELIEVER, WELCOME HIM INTO YOUR FELLOWSHIP, BUT NOT TO CRITICIZE HIS OPINIONS OR PASS JUDGMENT ON HIS SCRUPLES OR PERPLEX HIM WITH DISCUSSIONS. ONE MAN'S FAITH PERMITS HIM TO BELIEVE HE MAY EAT ANYTHING, WHILE A WEAKER ONE LIMITS HIS EATING TO VEGETABLES. LET NOT HIM WHO EATS LOOK DOWN ON OR DESPISE HIM WHO ABSTAINS AND LET NOT HIM WHO ABSTAINS CRITICIZE AND PASS JUDGMENT ON HIM WHO EATS; FOR GOD HAS ACCEPTED AND WELCOMED HIM (ROMANS 14:1-3)

Therefore if you serve God, how can you pass judgment on how another who also serves the Lord:

'IT IS BEFORE HIS OWN MASTER THAT HE STANDS OR FALLS, AND HE SHALL STAND AND BE UPHELD, FOR THE MASTER (THE LORD) IS MIGHTY TO SUPPORT HIM AND MAKE HIM STAND' (ROMANS 14:4).

Furthermore we are not to injure someone's conscience (despite their religious belief) for the sake of our own personal convictions, thus giving cause for others to criticize what is justifiable to us. This is especially for those who are more liberal in their walk with Christ.

To use the biblical example - you, who eat meat and drink wine, find occasion to be dining with someone who believes eating meat and drinking any alcohol to be morally wrong. If it is clear to you that that person would be offended by what you normally eat, then the right thing is to eat no meat or drink no wine or do anything else if it may cause an offense or create a stumbling block. Your personal convictions on such matters should be kept to yourself, exercised only in God's presence or in the company of those who share your convictions (Romans 14: 21).

You may say to yourself, 'why should I compromise my own convictions for the sake of someone else?' First of all, such an attitude is not in keeping with walking in love and would only lead to the ruin of one for whom Christ died for (Romans 14:15).

Secondly, this instruction is specifically for those whose convictions are more permissive than others. Let us turn this example around. You are the one who considers the eating of meat and the drinking of wine to be morally wrong. You find yourself dining with someone who eats and drinks without condemnation. Now if you follow his example, eating meat and drinking wine with an uneasy conscience, you bring yourself under condemnation before God because you are not true to your own convictions and therefore do not act from faith (Romans 14:23).

So you can see from this scripture how vital it is for those who are more accommodating in their beliefs to be sensitive and more responsible to those who have more restrictive beliefs. Furthermore no matter what your convictions none of us has the right to judge, criticize or condemn the other. When we serve Christ in this way we find acceptability to God and our fellow man (Romans 14:18).

For the purpose of strengthening our faith, I would like to highlight the fact that the bible does make a distinction between those who are strong in faith and those who are weak. Believers who are restricted or limited in their beliefs are considered to be weak in the faith (Romans 14: 1-2). Believer who have no such restraints and are liberated in their walk with Christ are considered to be strong in the faith. This viewpoint challenges what is widely perceived as strong faith.

Many believe their level of abstinence determines their level of faith. The more you are able to abstain, the more spiritual you are. The main reason for this level of abstinence is to make a clear distinction between what is considered worldly and unworldly. After all, the bible clearly states; 'be not conformed to this world' Romans

12:2). The problem is that many believers are not clear about what is worldly and what is unworldly and in our attempt to rid ourselves of all things worldly we tend to throw the baby out with the bath water. What has arisen is a belief that the way things are done in the church is God's way and anything else practiced outside of the church is deemed *worldly*.

Many high-level professionals who come to Christ have been accused of bringing their worldly ways into the church in their attempt to offer to the benefits of their experience. In so doing, many church leaders fail to realize that much of the principles and high standards practiced in the corporate world originate from devout men and women of God generations ago who were the founders of many of the institutions that we rely on today. To reject those same principles, labeling them as worldly, is to reject the work of God in the marketplace. God is a God of excellence and unfortunately the church lags behind when it comes to excellence.

The most widely held view in defining strong faith is tenacious belief. That is the ability to hold on to your beliefs, no matter what, in the face of adversity. This is what defines 'the Christian experience' - the test of our validity as true worshippers. This truly is a noble and necessary quality, but is a flawed perception, because it is possible to be wrong and strong! In other words you can hold on to a certain belief, one that you are willing to die for, that in the mind of God is irrelevant. Although it is vital to your faith to be true to your convictions, this does not define strong faith in its entirety.

So by what do we measure our level of faith? The answer is *clarity*. The strength of your faith is determined by a clear understanding of God and His Word. The division in beliefs highlighted by Paul, came about due to a lack of understanding of freedom in Christ. Those who are considered strong understand that there is nothing that is unclean (defiled or forbidden) in itself. Therefore they are not subject to the limitations of those who believe otherwise.

Obscurity of God's Word limits us and brings us into bondage. When you have clarity you have liberty and with liberty you have strength. As a matter of fact the more clarity you have about anything automatically gives you the winning edge.

HEAVEN'S MASTER KEY

Jesus said "I will give you (the church) the keys of the kingdom of heaven; and whatever you bind on earth must be what is already bound in heaven; and whatever you loose on earth must be what is already loosed in heaven" (Matthew 16:19).

The kingdom of heaven is like a house with many rooms each with a door. There's a medicine room for healing, a treasury for wealth and riches, a library for wisdom and knowledge, an artillery room for weaponry, a bedroom for peace and rest. In fact there's a room for everything you need in life; all you need is the right *key*. A key

◆FAITH

> IF YOU HAVE A RIGHT TO WHAT YOU ARE ASKING FOR THEN YOU DON'T NEED TO BEG!

is a device that enables the user to either gain access or to deny access. The keys of the kingdom of heaven will enable you to bind - that is to close or deny access, or loose, which refers to opening or gaining access. Usually in a house of many rooms there is need for a master key. A master key will allow you to operate many locks although each has its own key.

The kingdom of heaven has a master key, one that is simple but yet so powerful. It's all in the asking - I mean that literally, just ask! James 4:2 declares, *"You do not have because you do not ask."* Asking is the key to obtaining all that you desire.

Have you ever noticed that at times Jesus responded to questions with another question? For example when the disciples asked Jesus "where are we to get bread sufficient to feed so great a crowd in this desert?" His response was "how many loaves of bread do you have?" Jesus never asks questions in order to gain information because He already knows the answer (John 1:1). He asks in order to give us the questions we need to be asking. Therefore Jesus gave to His disciples the correct question they should ask. In this, He was revealing a Kingdom key that served in multiplying seven loaves and a few small fish to feed over 4000 people.

Now this is the confidence that we have in Him, that if we ask anything according to His will, He hears us. And if we know that He hears us, whatever we ask, we know that we have the petitions that we have asked of Him (1 John 5:14-15)

Questions are 'spiritual probes' which enable you to enquire, investigate and obtain things from God. Asking creates the shaft of a key. without its shaft a key cannot be inserted into the lock. Jesus' question about his true identity enabled Simon Peter to receive the revelation that 'Jesus is the Christ, the son of the living God' (Matthew 16:13-16). How do we receive wisdom? James says, *"if any of you lack wisdom, let him ask of God who gives to all men liberally..."* (James 1:5). Jesus said *"I will grant whatever you ask in my name"* (John 14:14). He also said "if you live in me and my words remains in you, ask whatever you will, and it shall be done for you" (John 15:7).

Picture a well, the type that has a bucket attached to a windup rope. By unwinding the rope the bucket is lowered down the well to draw up the water. In the same way, asking the right question allows you to go deep into your spirit and draw out the solution to your need. In Matthew 7:7 Jesus says, *"keep on asking and it will be given you; keep on seeking and you will find; keep on knocking and the door will be opened to you."* Seeking and knocking are just different forms of asking; but you have to be persistent at it. Why the need for persistence? Because the Kingdom only responds to a valid need or desire. Only faith can validate the request because faith cannot be faked. So we ask until we really believe in what we are asking for and in whom we require it from.

Prerequisites for Asking

There are prerequisites to our asking. First you must ask in faith. As mentioned you cannot fake faith. To ask in faith is to ask with a genuine confidence in:

1. The Giver
2. His ability to give
3. Your right to receive

These three factors are the essential elements of Heaven's master key. Doubt in any of these three areas will only serve to keep the windows of Heaven closed over your life. The third factor - your right to receive, is of great importance as it reflects on 'how' you ask. When you believe you have a right to what you are asking for, then you don't need to beg. It is not arrogant to live life with a sense of entitlement; after all, life does not give you what you deserve, only what you demand.

BUT LET HIM ASK IN FAITH, WITH NO DOUBTING, FOR HE WHO DOUBTS IS LIKE A WAVE OF THE SEA DRIVEN AND TOSSED BY THE WIND. FOR LET NOT THAT MAN SUPPOSE THAT HE WILL RECEIVE

ANYTHING FROM THE LORD (JAMES 1:6-7)

BUT WITHOUT FAITH IT IS IMPOSSIBLE TO PLEASE HIM, FOR HE WHO COMES TO GOD MUST BELIEVE THAT HE IS, AND THAT HE IS A REWARDER OF THOSE WHO DILIGENTLY SEEK HIM (HEBREWS 11:6).

Secondly, we must have the right motive:

YOU ASK AND YET FAIL TO RECEIVE, BECAUSE YOU ASK WITH WRONG PURPOSE AND EVIL, SELFISH MOTIVES (JAMES 4:3)

Why are you asking for what you are asking? That is the question we all must ask ourselves. The answer to this is not as obvious as it seems, especially when we keep probing through the layers of excuses that mask our real intentions. Jesus said:

"IF YOU ABIDE IN ME, AND MY WORDS ABIDE IN YOU, YOU WILL ASK WHAT YOU DESIRE, AND IT SHALL BE DONE FOR YOU" (JOHN 15:7).

This simply means that when we share His heart and adopt His way of thinking, the Kingdom of Heaven will respond to all that we ask for.

Last (but, by no means least) Matthew 7:7-12 reveals a vital connection to receiving what we ask. After mentioning persistence in asking, seeking and knocking, He gives this illustration:

✢FAITH

"What man is there of you, if his son asks him for a loaf of bread, will hand him a stone? Or if he asks for a fish, will hand him a serpent? If you then, evil as you are, know how to give good gifts to your children, how much more will your heavenly Father give good gifts to those who keep on asking him! So then, whatever you desire others to do and for you, even so do also to and for them, for this sums up the law and the prophets."

The law and the prophets make up the whole of the old testament, which is the foundation of the new testament. Jesus teaches us that God's laws and commandments can be summed up as 'doing unto others as you would have them do unto you.' When we develop a track record of treating others as we want to be treated, we will have no problem receiving what we ask from God because we have proved that our motives are good. Proverbs 18:24 KJV says, *"…a man that hath friends must show himself friendly."*

A principle related to this can be found in the new testament: "whatever a man sows, that and only that is what he will reap." (Galatians 6:7). We should treat others with the same sincerity that we would (should) for our children. Jesus made the comparison between the bread (Hebrew style) and stone because they were similar in appearance. This is also true for the fish and the serpent. This communicates the difference between giving someone the genuine article and an imitation.

For example, if your spouse or child(ren) needs your time, give them quality time not just your presence. If you are buying someone a gift, buy something of quality that you would want for yourself (budget allowing). Don't let the phrase 'it's the thought that counts' be a substitute for giving your best!

The ability to effectively treat others as we want to be treated depends on your own self worth. One of the great commandments upon which all the commandments depend on is 'love your neighbor as you do yourself' (Matthew 22:39). Your love for yourself is critical and affects your relationship with others. Failure to love yourself is disobedience to one of God's greatest commands! 1 John 4:19 says, *"we love him because he first loved us"* - we can truly love ourselves when we recognize God's love for us. The more you recognize his love for you, the more you will love yourself. The more you love yourself the better you should love others.

Do unto others as you would have them do unto you. Not only will you reap the harvest of what you have sown, but you will receive what you desire - only if you ask.

❖FAITH

THE KINGDOM

✽THE KINGDOM

KINGDOM 101

With what can we compare the Kingdom of God, or what parable shall we use to illustrate and explain it? It is like a grain of mustard seed, which when sown upon the ground, is the smallest of all seeds upon the earth; yet after it is sown, it grows up and becomes the greatest of all garden herbs and puts out large branches, so that the birds of the air are able to make nests and dwell in its shade. Mark 4:30-32.

The above text illustrates the dynamics of the Kingdom of God. It is based on sowing seed and seeing the manifestation of what you have sown. Previous to the above text Jesus gives a similar illustration:

IGNORANCE IS ROBBING YOU OF WHAT YOU COULD HAVE

"SO IS THE KINGDOM OF GOD, AS IF A MAN SHOULD CAST SEED INTO THE GROUND, AND SHOULD SLEEP, AND RISE NIGHT AND DAY, AND THE SEED SHOULD SPRING AND GROW UP, HE KNOWETH NOT HOW" (MARK 4:26-27)

Parables are loaded with symbolic representation. In order for us to have greater understanding of this concept as it relates to the Kingdom of God we must be able to decode the symbols used in these parables.

In Marks account of the parable of the sower (Mark 4:1-9), Jesus' disciples asked Him to explain the meaning of the parable. His response was *"do you not understand this parable? How then will you understand all the parables?"* In other words when we understand the parable of the sower and what the symbols represent we have the key to understanding all other parables related to the Kingdom of God. Lets us look at the parable and the symbols used in the parable of the sower with their meanings as explained by Jesus:

BEHOLD, THERE WENT OUT A SOWER TO SOW: AND IT CAME TO PASS, AS HE SOWED, SOME FELL BY THE WAY SIDE, AND THE FOWLS OF THE AIR CAME AND DEVOURED IT UP. AND SOME FELL ON STONY GROUND, WHERE IT HAD NOT MUCH EARTH; AND IMMEDIATELY IT SPRANG UP, BECAUSE IT HAD NO DEPTH OF EARTH: BUT WHEN THE SUN WAS UP, IT WAS SCORCHED; AND BECAUSE IT HAD NO ROOT, IT WITHERED AWAY. AND SOME FELL AMONG THORNS, AND THE

THORNS GREW UP, AND CHOKED IT, AND IT YIELDED NO FRUIT. AND OTHER FELL ON GOOD GROUND, AND DID YIELD FRUIT THAT SPRANG UP AND INCREASED; AND BROUGHT FORTH, SOME THIRTY, AND SOME SIXTY, AND SOME AN HUNDRED (MARK 4:1-9)

According to Jesus' explanation of this parable, here are the key symbols and their meaning:

SEED - seeds are containers of reproductive components. Jesus likened seeds to the Word. God's words are spiritual containers of faith. Hebrews 11:3 says, *"through faith we understand that the worlds were framed by the Word of God, so that things which are seen were not made of things which do appear."* Faith is the reproductive and creative power used to create all things.

It is crucial to this whole subject to clarify what is the Word. The Greek word used for Word here is *logos*. Logos amongst other definitions means thought, intelligence and reasoning. Logos embraces an ideology or way of thinking. In Matthew's account of the parable of the sower, Jesus makes specific reference to the 'Word of the Kingdom' (Matthew 13:19). In other words He is talking about Kingdom thinking. From the parables that Jesus uses to describe the Kingdom of God, we can see that Kingdom thinking embraces increase, achievement, blessings and success. These are the outflow of God's love. Our comprehension of this vital truth is key to understanding the operation of God's Kingdom.

GROUND - the ground represents the heart of man. The heart (not the physical organ) is the center of man's thoughts, emotions and actions. It pertains to his character, beliefs, values and attitude to life. It is only through the heart of a man that manifestation takes places hence the writer says, *"keep thy heart with all diligence; for out of it are the issues of life"* (Proverbs 4:23). The condition of your heart is of vital importance if there is to be manifestation. This is seen in the 4 types of ground illustrated by Jesus:

The wayside - the heart that does not accommodate Kingdom thinking

Stony ground - the heart that does not have the depth of character to maintain or hold onto Kingdom thinking.

Thorny ground - the heart that is consumed with the cares of the world and is easily distracted.

Good soil - the heart that accommodates, acts on and comprehends Kingdom thinking which in turn yields fruit.

FRUIT - fruit represents the manifestation of what was sown. It is the evidence of your faith or in business terms, is the return on your investment.

YIELD - the amount of fruit produced.

These are the same key elements used in our opening text. Therefore the Kingdom of God works on the principle of getting the Word into your heart and then seeing the manifestation of that Word in your life.

How do we get the Word in our hearts? Romans 10:17 says, *"faith cometh by hearing and hearing by the Word of God."* There are two types of hearing: outer and inner hearing. In this context, outer hearing pertains to the Word we hear audibly, either from other people or by speaking the Word to ourselves (positive confessions). However, inner hearing pertains to our 'self talk' or our dominant thoughts. Jesus says on numerous occasions "he who has ears to hear, let him hear." What you are hearing on the inside is critical to manifesting the power of faith. Your positive declarations must be congruent with your internal dialogue.

We may hear the Word externally first of all, however, we must continue hearing that Word internally. When we continue to hear the Word internally it becomes our thoughts. When it becomes our thoughts it then moves into the realm of imagination. Genesis 11:6 says, *"...nothing will be restrained from them, which they have imagined to do."* Therefore whatever is held in our imagination long enough becomes manifestation.

Not only do we want to bear fruit, we also want lots of it (yield). Jesus said, *"the fruit sprang up and increased and brought forth some thirty, and some sixty and some a hundred fold."* (Mark 4:8). A useful question to ask is do we have any control to how much we fruit we yield and if so what determines how much we can yield? The answer to that question is found in Mark 4:24;

"BE CAREFUL WHAT YOU ARE HEARING. THE MEASURE OF THOUGHT AND STUDY YOU GIVE TO THE TRUTH YOU HEAR WILL BE THE MEASURE OF VIRTUE AND KNOWLEDGE THAT COMES BACK TO YOU - AND MORE BESIDES WILL BE GIVEN TO YOU WHO HEAR."

Simply put 'the more you learn, the more you earn'. The more knowledge you have, the more you will achieve. If you want to yield a hundred fold then you need 100% understanding of what you want to manifest. You won't get the hundred fold with 30% knowledge! Proverbs 3:19 states; *'the Lord by wisdom hath founded the earth; by understanding hath he established the heavens.'* Wisdom and understanding are the very foundation of God's Kingdom. In Hebrew thinking, light represents knowledge whereas darkness represents ignorance. Ignorance is robbing you of what you could have. Hence the writer urges us to 'get wisdom and with all your getting, get understanding' (Proverbs 4:7).

GREATER THAN MY ROOTS

"The kingdom of heaven is like to a grain of mustard seed, which a man took, and sowed in his field. Which indeed is the least of all seeds: but when it is grown, it is the greatest among herbs, and becometh a tree, so that the birds of the air come and lodge in the branches thereof" Matthew 13: 31-32 KJV

Breaking Barriers

Typically by nature, every living thing reproduces after it's own kind. Apples contain seed which when sown will develop into an apple tree. Same with oranges,

> PURPOSE IS NEVER THRUST ONTO THE UNPREPARED

tomatoes, pears and the like. We do not expect anything more from an apple seed other than more apples.

In general we tend to have the same attitude in our expectation of individuals, especially within the context of race, gender, status and class. Although not readily seen we live in a world with many barriers. There are social barriers and taboos, racial barriers, glass ceilings, societal expectations, cult-ural expectations, religious expectations and a raft of other barriers that many of us tend to live with. Worst still are our own self limiting expectations that we have learned to accept.

Although we live in unprecedented times, where there are more self made millionaires than any other time before, there is still a trend as to what things certain types of people will become successful at. For example we see many African Americans become very successful in the field of sport and entertainment, but how many are at the helm of fortune 500 companies or even fortune 1000? In a world of equality only 15 fortune 500 companies are currently run by women. The reason for this may be found not only by the glass ceiling that exists through every sector of society but also in the limitations of our own aspirations.

We tend to model our aspirations around those that look like us, talk like us or come from the same environment as us. Thus we emulate the same concept of reproducing after our own kind. You may not see this as an issue, after all, we are all creatures of nature and thus subject to the laws of nature. However, if that is the case, why do we possess the potential to do so much more. An apple will only produce more apples, nothing more. Each of us on the other hand are uniquely created to do what no-one else has done before. Each of us possess the ability to break barriers that no-one else thought could be broken.

Then there is the question of what we would do when we reach the top of our profession? What happens when we have achieved our goals? When we have achieved all of what was expected of us, what happens next?

The Beginning of Greatness

In Jesus' teachings, the mustard seed is often used to symbolize the nature of the Kingdom, where the very least is all that is required to achieve what was considered impossible.

"I SAY TO YOU, IF YOU HAVE FAITH AS A MUSTARD SEED, YOU WILL SAY TO THIS MOUNTAIN, 'MOVE FROM HERE TO THERE,' AND IT WILL MOVE; AND NOTHING WILL BE IMPOSSIBLE FOR YOU" (MATTHEW 17:20)

◆THE KINGDOM

When you understand the Kingdom, you will realize that how much you have to start with is never a problem. Knowing what to do with the little that you have is the key to achieving what you want.

That evening the disciples came to him and said, "This is a desolate place, and it is getting late. Send the crowds away so they can go to the villages and buy food for themselves." But Jesus replied, "That isn't necessary - you feed them." "Impossible!" they exclaimed. "We have only five loaves of bread and two fish!" "Bring them here," he said. Then he told the people to sit down on the grass. And he took the five loaves and two fish, looked up toward heaven, and asked God's blessing on the food. Breaking the loaves into pieces, he gave some of the bread and fish to each disciple, and the disciples gave them to the people. They all ate as much as they wanted, and they picked up twelve baskets of leftovers. About five thousand men had eaten from those five loaves, in addition to all the women and children! (Matthew 14: 15-21 NLT)

Here we see Jesus using the Kingdom principle of the very least being used to achieve what was considered impossible. He did the same thing again when he fed four thousand from seven loaves and a few small fish (Matthew 15:33-39). This principle is not exclusive to Jesus alone. Elijah used it when he caused a widow and her son to be sustained throughout a long drought from just a handful of flour and a small amount of oil (1 Kings 17:7-16). His successor, Elisha, used the same principle when he helped another widow out of debt by enabling her to sell many vessels of oil from just one jar of oil (2 Kings 4:1-6).

A principle will work for anyone who understands how to execute it.

The Power to become Great

We live in an extremely potent universe where every atom is packed with unimaginable power. This fact was realized through the genius of Albert Einstein. Regarded as the father of modern physics, his most well-known accomplishment is the relativity formula $E=mc^2$. Despite its familiarity, many people don't really understand what it means.

According to Einstein, matter (mass) and energy are really just different forms of the same thing. Matter can be converted into energy and energy into matter. In one kilogram of pure water, the mass of hydrogen atoms amounts to just slightly more than 111 grams, or 0.111 kg. Einstein's formula tells us the amount of energy this mass would be equivalent to, if it were all suddenly turned into energy.

The energy (E) is found by multiplying the mass (M) by the square of the speed of light (C). The speed of light is 300,000,000 meters per second thus our calculation for energy from 0.111Kg of water looks like this:

$E=mc^2$
$= 0.111 \times 300,000,000 \times 300,000,000$
$= 10,000,000,000,000,000$ joules (joules being the unit of energy)

That is an incredible amount of energy! 30 grammes of water seems insignificant, but if you knew how to convert that into energy you would have the equivalent of more than one hundred thousand gallons of burning gasoline!

So we are all immersed in an environment of immeasurable energy all of which is at our disposal if we know how to harness it. The key to harnessing anything is the understanding of the laws by which it operates or responds to. Everything is governed by laws. The invention of the light bulb, radio, TV etc came about through discovering the laws by which these things operate. Many of these laws (usually expressed in mathematic format) have been named after the scientist who discovered them; such as Newton's law of gravity, Faradays law of electromagnetic induction and the fore-mentioned theory of relativity by Albert Einstein.

But how does all this relate to our personal circumstances? To answer this question you must have a wider understanding of what energy is. Energy is not limited to that which fuels our cars, homes, towns and cities. Neither is it limited to that which fuels and sustains our bodies. Energy is also the product of mental activity. To put it another way, your thoughts have power! Not only does your thoughts have power to determine your feelings and your actions, but also to affect your circumstances and the circumstances of others. Thus situations and circumstances are the product of thoughts. The situation you are in now was caused by thoughts, whether it be your own or the system of thinking held by those around you, your community or even your country.

The power to change our circumstances responds only to spiritual and mental laws. Therefore, the laws that govern situations and circumstances are both spiritual and mental. These laws are rooted in the most powerful and empowering belief system; namely faith. Faith is the key to harnessing the power that is able to change our circumstances and propel us in the direction of our own aspirations.

Faith is not about religion nor should it be relegated to it! Faith is about exercising the ability to realize our full potential and overcome any obstacle that comes in our way.

Recognizing a seed

Armed with this knowledge, we should no longer see the limitations of our present circumstances as a reason why we cannot achieve whatever we want in life. On the contrary, like the mustard seed in the opening parable, humble circumstances serve only as the seed that will grow into greatness. Greatness begins with the recognition of what you have. Unfortunately many of us overlook what we have or believe we do not have anything at all. However, the notion of having nothing is really just a failure to recognize the existence of something you already possess. We must understand that having nothing is an impossibility! In the same way Adam was able to name and thus define anything that God presented to him, we too are able to define whatever we have or whatever is presented to us. Once something is defined it then becomes recognizable.

When you recognize something it takes on the form and function of what you defined it to be. Thus through recognition you have the power to create the seed that will propel you to greatness. Seeds can be ideas, money, circumstances, talents, even a website and a host of other things just waiting for your recognition to kick start the process of manifestation.

Paying The Price
(putting first things first)

Once you have your seed you must energize it with your faith. In practical terms this entails making decisions and carrying out actions based on your belief and confidence in what the Kingdom can achieve with your seed. Your faith is displayed through your willingness to pay the price for the fulfillment of what you want to achieve. The widow Elijah helped through the drought paid the price of faith by giving him her last meal. It was a meal intend for herself and her son before they faced certain death from starvation. Instead she fore-went her portion and gave it to the prophet instead (and most probably her son too). Jesus fed the five thousand because a boy gave the five loaves and two small fish that he had.

Paying the price should not be seen as a tariff the Kingdom charges for it's solutions. It's about putting first things first. One of the biggest causes of failure is misplaced priorities. It is an unfortunate fact that the biggest consumers in the world are not the rich, but the poor. When I say poor, I am referring to the working and middle class. The rich are always looking for ways to invest their money. The poor take the little that they have and spend it. The rich uses loans as leverage to get more money. The poor take out loans to spend it and get deeper into debt. As mentioned, the little that you have is your seed. Seed is meant to be sown, not eaten. At first glance it might've seem unfair for Elijah to have taken the widow woman's last meal, but if he had not been there, this woman, along with her son, would have eaten her 'seed' and then died.

Putting first things first is fundamental to getting what you need in life and even more so in the kingdom:

So why do you worry about clothing? Consider the lilies of the field, how they grow: they neither toil nor spin; and yet I say to you that even Solomon in all his glory was not arrayed like one of these. Now if God so clothes the grass of the field, which today is, and tomorrow is thrown into the oven, will He not much more clothe you, O you of little faith? Therefore do not worry, saying, 'What shall we eat?' or 'What shall we drink?' or 'What shall we wear?' For after all these things the Gentiles seek. For your heavenly Father knows that you need all these things. But seek first the kingdom of God and His righteousness, and all these things shall be added to you (Matthew 6:28-33)

Like the widow who gave the prophet her last meal, or the boy who gave Jesus the fish and the loaves, the seriousness of your faith is proven only by your decision to prioritize the Kingdom above your immediate needs. Greatness comes at a cost and you must be willing to pay the price with your time, energy, emotions and resources in order to bring your plans to fruition.

Sowing the seed

As in nature, it is crucial that you sow your seed in the right soil. In Jesus' parable of the sower, He explained that the seed in this case was the word of the Kingdom and the different soils the seeds fell on represented various heart conditions. When the bible speaks of the heart it is referring to the mind. The good soil that yielded the harvest was the mind that was able to comprehend the word of the Kingdom. It is the quality of your mind that determines the quality of your life. There is no better investment you can make than that which improves the quality of your mind. Your mind is the interface between the little that you have now and greater you will have. You will only have greater, however, if your mind serves as an asset and not a liability. Your mind will only be an asset to you, when you feed it with the mental protein it requires to nourish your life. This mental protein is called is wisdom. Wisdom is the application of knowledge. To apply knowledge effectively requires understanding. Greatness, therefore, requires a staple diet of wisdom, knowledge and understanding.

HAPPY IS THE MAN WHO FINDS WISDOM, AND THE MAN WHO GAINS UNDERSTANDING; FOR HER PROCEEDS ARE BETTER THAN THE PROFITS OF SILVER, AND HER GAIN THAN FINE GOLD. SHE IS MORE PRECIOUS THAN RUBIES, AND ALL THE THINGS YOU MAY DESIRE CANNOT COMPARE WITH HER. LENGTH OF DAYS IS IN HER

RIGHT HAND, IN HER LEFT HAND RICHES AND HONOR. HER WAYS ARE WAYS OF PLEASANTNESS, AND ALL HER PATHS ARE PEACE. SHE IS A TREE OF LIFE TO THOSE WHO TAKE HOLD OF HER, AND HAPPY ARE ALL WHO RETAIN HER. THE LORD BY WISDOM FOUNDED THE EARTH; BY UNDERSTANDING HE ESTABLISHED THE HEAVENS; BY HIS KNOWLEDGE THE DEPTHS WERE BROKEN UP, AND CLOUDS DROP DOWN THE DEW. (PROVERBS 3:13-21)

MY SON, IF YOU RECEIVE MY WORDS, AND TREASURE MY COMMANDS WITHIN YOU, SO THAT YOU INCLINE YOUR EAR TO WISDOM, AND APPLY YOUR HEART TO UNDERSTANDING; YES, IF YOU CRY OUT FOR DISCERNMENT, AND LIFT UP YOUR VOICE FOR UNDERSTANDING, IF YOU SEEK HER AS SILVER, AND SEARCH FOR HER AS FOR HIDDEN TREASURES; THEN YOU WILL UNDERSTAND THE FEAR OF THE LORD, AND FIND THE KNOWLEDGE OF GOD. FOR THE LORD GIVES WISDOM; FROM HIS MOUTH COME KNOWLEDGE AND UNDERSTANDING. (PROVERBS 2:1-6)

Putting miracles in perspective

From Heaven's perspective, the Kingdom functions by wisdom, knowledge and understanding, not by miracles! Miracles are actions that only appear miraculous with the absence of knowing the laws by which they function by. In other words they are actions using laws that are unknown to us. Imagine a man from the 10th century entering into our present time. What is normal for us would be miraculous to him. He may even believe we are gods! In the same way, what appears as miracles to us are not miracles in Heaven. Although many of the miracles illustrated in the bible defy the laws of nature, they still occur through laws, albeit spiritual laws that have the ability to supersede physical laws.

Miracles usually occur in times of crisis. A crisis only exists when the solution to a critical problem is beyond our reach. Therefore a miracle can be seen as an intervention by God to provide a solution that only He can provide at the time. Here lies the critical reason why we must be clear on the role of miracles. IF the solution already exists then there is no need for a miracle! Unfortunately there are those who are unable to accept this simple truth due to their rejection of man-made solutions and their insistence on the miraculous. For example there are those who reject modern medicine at the insistence of receiving divine healing. There are those who reject the sound wisdom of professionals and industry field leaders at the insistence of purely miraculous ways of overcoming problems and advancing in life. However, this way of thinking serves only to impede progress rather than advance it. This is because with this attitude miracles become a crutch and resolves you of your responsibility in obtaining the wisdom, knowledge, skills and understanding necessary for you to advance in life.

Wisdom and the solutions that comes from it are only 'discovered' by men who search for what has been concealed by God:

IF ANY OF YOU LACKS WISDOM, LET HIM ASK OF GOD, WHO GIVES TO ALL LIBERALLY AND WITHOUT REPROACH, AND IT WILL BE GIVEN TO HIM (JAMES 1:5)

IT IS THE GLORY OF GOD TO CONCEAL A MATTER, BUT THE GLORY OF KINGS IS TO SEARCH OUT A MATTER (PROVERBS 25:2)

God conceals things, not to keep us in ignorance, but that it might be revealed in the right time and to the right generation. There are solutions available to us now that were not available to the previous generation. Therefore there was a reliance in the miraculous in certain things that was necessary for the previous generations. However, where wisdom abounds there is no need for the miraculous to occur unless it should be for God's own reasons for revealing Himself in that particular way. Holding onto beliefs and practices that were necessary for past generations but are no longer necessary for us now, will only serve to align ourselves with a way of life that resists change and hinders progress. The rejection of solutions discovered by men for the reasons of receiving from God instead, is in reality a rejection of what God has already provided. If a miracle should occur in this event it is only because ignorance has created a crisis that God chooses to deal with out of compassion. However, God wants us to live blessed rather than by miracles. To be blessed is to be empowered to prosper. Wisdom, knowledge and understanding are the greatest empowerments for prosperity.

By no means am I saying that miracles are no longer relevant. In our walk of faith there will always be gaps in what we know and what we can do that requires divine intervention to assist us. This is likened to parents teaching their child to walk. The parent's goal is for the child to be able to walk unassisted; however, they will standby ready to intervene when that child inevitably falls from trying to take those first steps. Over time the child will be able to take more strides before stumbling. Then there will be a time when the child can walk unaided. The joy of any parent is to see their child walking without having to be assisted. No good parent wants to constantly help a child to walk!

Recognizing the Kingdom at work

The reason why it is so important to understand the role of miracles is because the bible illustrates the workings of the Kingdom in a very spectacular and miraculous way. However, the world we live in today is far removed from how it was in the ancient world. As explained, what was necessary back then is not what is totally necessary today. If we focus on the miracles we will be none the wiser on how the Kingdom operates. Therefore when we study the workings of the kingdom in the bible it is important to recognize the principles and patterns at work rather than the miracles themselves. Principles and patterns are oblivious to the passage of time and remain relevant regardless of changing circumstances. The principles (keys) of the Kingdom have both a spiritual and natural correlation:

I WILL GIVE YOU THE KEYS OF THE KINGDOM OF HEAVEN, AND WHATEVER YOU BIND ON EARTH WILL BE BOUND IN HEAVEN, AND WHATEVER YOU LOOSE ON EARTH WILL BE LOOSED IN HEAVEN" (MATTHEW 16:19)

Both the Heavenly (spiritual) and the natural realms are of equal relevance to one another. Neither realm functions independently of the other. Things physical are made from things spiritual and things that occur in the natural has an unseen yet real effect in the spiritual realm. Therefore physical/natural achievement should be given the same divine accreditation as that which was achieved supernaturally. Failure to do this will result in a failure to recognize divine opportunities.

Recognizing the dual nature of the Kingdom is a critical component in the realization of our full potential. Not only is this important from a universal perspective but also from a personal one. This is because the Kingdom functions from within us rather than without (Luke 17:21). We were all designed with the same dual dynamics as the Kingdom; that is having both a spiritual and physical function. Animals do not have this function neither do plants. Only the human mind has the ability to translate between the spiritual realm and the natural. This is a divine ability and apart from God we are the only vessels in the universe with the capacity to embody the Kingdom in this way.

Not only can we embody the Kingdom, we can also emulate the Kingdom. Thus the great feats illustrated and performed in the bible is merely an expression of what can be performed and reflected in our lives. The Kingdom therefore is our birth right and it's presence in us is proof of our divine relationship as sons and heirs of God.

Facilitating Increase

Like the mustard seed that grows to become a tree in our opening parable, greatness too is a process of growth. As mentioned, the feats performed in the bible serves as an expression of what can be done in our lives. Increase is the signature piece of the Kingdom. It is characteristic of many of the feats recorded in the bible. However, there is a particular way increase occurs that reoccurs when the principles of increase are in operation. To see an example of this let's look at Luke's account of how Jesus fed five thousand in the wilderness:

WHEN THE DAY BEGAN TO WEAR AWAY, THE TWELVE CAME AND SAID TO HIM, "SEND THE MULTITUDE AWAY, THAT THEY MAY GO INTO THE SURROUNDING TOWNS AND COUNTRY, AND LODGE AND

✳THE KINGDOM

GET PROVISIONS; FOR WE ARE IN A DESERTED PLACE HERE." BUT HE SAID TO THEM, "YOU GIVE THEM SOMETHING TO EAT." AND THEY SAID, "WE HAVE NO MORE THAN FIVE LOAVES AND TWO FISH, UNLESS WE GO AND BUY FOOD FOR ALL THESE PEOPLE." FOR THERE WERE ABOUT FIVE THOUSAND MEN. THEN HE SAID TO HIS DISCIPLES, "MAKE THEM SIT DOWN IN GROUPS OF FIFTY." AND THEY DID SO, AND MADE THEM ALL SIT DOWN. THEN HE TOOK THE FIVE LOAVES AND THE TWO FISH, AND LOOKING UP TO HEAVEN, HE BLESSED AND BROKE THEM, AND GAVE THEM TO THE DISCIPLES TO SET BEFORE THE MULTITUDE. SO THEY ALL ATE AND WERE FILLED, AND TWELVE BASKETS OF THE LEFTOVER FRAGMENTS WERE TAKEN UP BY THEM (LUKE 9:12-17).

First it should be noted that in John's account of this event, Jesus blessed the food by simply giving thanks. All of us are capable of showing gratitude and giving thanks. I make this point for you to realize that nothing here was done that is beyond the capability of anyone who is willing to put their trust and faith in the Kingdom. Often time the Kingdom is portrayed as something only accessible to the spiritual elite and those claiming a higher moral standing that gives them the right and ability to exercise the power of the kingdom. However, Jesus declared that *"the Kingdom suffers violence and the violent take it by force"* (Matthew 11:12). The violent refers to people of strong conviction and determination, who will not capitulate to the antagonism of their situation, but rather, take hold with full entitlement, the blessings and abundance of the Kingdom.

Secondly, He made the multitude sit in fifties before the bread and fish could be distributed to them. In other words, He made them get organized so they can receive the food. The importance being organized cannot be emphasized enough as this is a crucial stage in the process of increase.

Getting organized involves putting a system or structure in place in order for activities or work to be done more effectively. The better the structure, the more work can be done and the more work you will get the opportunity to. God blesses structure. He does not pour out His blessings on anything that will not facilitate it:

Honor the Lord with your possessions, And with the firstfruits of all your increase; So your barns will be filled with plenty, And your vats will overflow with new wine (Proverbs 3:9-10)

The Lord will command the blessing on you in your storehouses and in all to which you set your hand, and He will bless you in the land which the Lord your God is giving you (Deuteronomy 28:8)

As agriculture was central to the economy of the Israelites, barns and storehouses were as important to them as banks are to us today. Barns and storehouses represent the structure they used to facilitate their survival and growth. Any business, institution or individual that does not have a structure or an organized way of doing things will not be able to facilitate growth. No matter how much income you earn, if you have no system in place to manage it, you will find yourself in lack. When the widow came to Elisha for help in preventing the creditors from taking her sons into slavery he said to her:

"WHAT SHALL I DO FOR YOU? TELL ME, WHAT DO YOU HAVE IN THE HOUSE?" AND SHE SAID, "YOUR MAIDSERVANT HAS NOTHING IN THE HOUSE BUT A JAR OF OIL." GO, BORROW VESSELS FROM EVERYWHERE, FROM ALL YOUR NEIGHBORS - EMPTY VESSELS; DO NOT GATHER JUST A FEW. AND WHEN YOU HAVE COME IN, YOU SHALL SHUT THE DOOR BEHIND YOU AND YOUR SONS; THEN POUR IT INTO ALL THOSE VESSELS, AND SET ASIDE THE FULL ONES." SO SHE WENT FROM HIM AND SHUT THE DOOR BEHIND HER AND HER SONS, WHO BROUGHT THE VESSELS TO HER; AND SHE POURED IT OUT. NOW IT CAME TO PASS, WHEN THE VESSELS WERE FULL, THAT SHE SAID TO HER SON, "BRING ME ANOTHER VESSEL." AND HE SAID TO HER, "THERE IS NOT ANOTHER VESSEL." SO THE OIL CEASED (2 KINGS 4:3-6)

Elisha had the woman put a system in place to facilitate the increase of oil. As long as there were vessels the oil kept pouring. The only reason the oil ceased was because there were no more vessels to pour into. Here lies a very important lesson, the only thing that will limit what the Kingdom can provide for you is your ability to facilitate it. There is no reason why the widow could not have been selling oil for the rest of her life if she focused her efforts on getting more vessels. Think of the wealth she could have accumulated for herself, her sons and for their children, if only she had exercised foresight and elicit the services of a potter to provide a steady supply of vessels!

Structure is key to converting what you have to what you need. If you are experiencing lack, where once you had abundance, take a good look at your structure. Do you have systems in place to facilitate changes in the way business is done? Have you considered the structure of the different areas of your life, i.e. social, professional, family and spiritual? All of these areas are interlinked and interdependent on one another and you should therefore structure your life with this in mind.

There can be no progress or success without structure. The world has an abundance of talented and gifted people, but the main reason why many of these talented people are not successful is primarily due to the lack of structure. Imagine a bodybuilder with rippling muscles everywhere! Now imagine how that bodybuilder would look without a skeleton! Quite an ugly sight I would imagine. A mass of muscles without the ability to do anything! In principle this is the case when you have talent but no structure. You're gifted but without structure you will go nowhere.

Structure is a reflection of the way you think.
Jesus said:

#THE KINGDOM

"NO ONE PUTS NEW WINE INTO OLD WINESKINS; OR ELSE THE NEW WINE BURSTS THE WINESKINS, THE WINE IS SPILLED, AND THE WINESKINS ARE RUINED. BUT NEW WINE MUST BE PUT INTO NEW WINESKINS" (MARK 2:22)

He said this in addressing the difference between the thinking of the religious and the thinking of the Kingdom. Likewise, if your thinking is incongruent with the principles of wealth, then you will not be able experience wealth or increase without consequence.

How Increase works

Looking again at when Jesus fed the five thousand, there was never a time when five thousand fish and loaves was readily available for distribution. There was no great stock pile out of which the food was distributed. The increase occurred step by step, bit by bit as the food was broken and distributed. Each piece was broken and given in faith believing there would be more from where that came from. From a Kingdom perspective, faith should never be placed in the abundance you can see. Your faith should be in source from whence abundance comes; namely the Kingdom. This was also the case with the widow and the oil that filled the vessels. Each of those large vessels were filled to the brim from the same small jar of oil.

The path to greatness is a sequence of small leaps of faith. There are no stepping stones laid out before you except for that which only you can see by faith. Therefore each leap you take is done believing the stone will appear in time to support your feet. Such is the way of the Kingdom, a walk by faith and not by sight. However, it is not a walk for the blind, but those with vision. As long as you have made the mental, physical, spiritual and organizational preparation required for each step towards your vision, there is no reason for the stepping stone not to appear.

Transformation

BUT WHEN IT IS GROWN, IT IS THE GREATEST AMONG HERBS, AND BECOMETH A TREE, SO THAT THE BIRDS OF THE AIR COME AND LODGE IN THE BRANCHES THEREOF (MATTHEW 13:32)

So now you are nearing the end game, as your walk of faith has taken you through many barriers and elevated you to higher levels. From your humble beginnings you are now head and shoulders with those whom you looked up to. You're at the height of your profession and respected amongst your peers. You have experienced unprecedented increase and now you are living the dream. Like the apple seed that becomes an apple, indeed now you are the greatest amongst herbs as your seed, the smallest of all seeds, comes into fruition. From your lofty

◆THE KINGDOM

position you are an inspiration to those amongst whom you came from. However, from your lofty position you are now confronted with the proverbial glass ceiling as aspirations beyond what you had dreamed of now come to bare. Although this is a glass ceiling accepted by your contemporaries, something inside you is tugging at your heart relentlessly, urging you to go beyond.

No one would blame you for staying where you are, after all you are already a role model to many. Besides, as already mentioned, everything produces after it's own kind and you are the embodiment of that. It is truly inspiring in itself that you have reached where you are, the greatest among herbs. However, in the grand scheme of things, herbs, exist at the feet of trees and according to the parable you are yet to become a tree.

Here's the problem - by nature, mustard seeds do not grow into trees. As a matter of fact, there is no such thing as a mustard tree! A mustard becomes a plant or a shrub at best, but not a tree. A full grown mustard plant will not support the weight of birds coming to nest in its branches nor will it provide any shade. Is this an oversight in the parable or a contradiction in terms? Maybe Jesus' botanical knowledge was lacking in some places? No, there is no error in Jesus' words and it would be of great benefit to note at this point that whenever we come across what seems to be a contradiction in the bible is really an opportunity for revelation of a deeper truth. As long as we hold on to the fact that there is no contradiction or error in the bible and keep probing, that hidden nugget will be revealed to us.

The only way for a herb to become a tree is through transformation. It's a transformation from within expressed as a transfiguration without. Like Jesus being transfigured on the mount of olives, each of us must experience our own transfiguration where we become something greater than what are roots implied.

Transfiguration is the time when you really start to shine and your beauty is revealed. This will only take place when you answer the call of that which continues to tug at your heart. When you are willing to go into uncharted territory and explore potential your contemporaries failed to explore, that is when you become ripe for transfiguration.

Although Jesus had accomplish much, His transfiguration did not take place until further on in His ministry just before what was to be the very crux of His mission. Likewise your journey will bring you to a point where you will realize that everything you did before was just preparation for what now lies ahead. Purpose is never thrust onto the unprepared.

As mentioned, transfiguration is when you begin to shine and reveal your true beauty. This is what literally took place in Jesus' case:

> NOW AFTER SIX DAYS JESUS TOOK PETER, JAMES, AND JOHN HIS BROTHER, LED THEM UP ON A HIGH MOUNTAIN BY THEMSELVES; 2 AND HE WAS TRANSFIGURED BEFORE THEM. HIS FACE SHONE LIKE THE SUN, AND HIS CLOTHES BECAME AS WHITE AS THE LIGHT (MATTHEW 17:1-7)

Your transfiguration will happen in a manner that is apt for who you are and what your purpose is. Transfiguration can come in a form of a renewed attitude and a change of image. When I say change of image, I mean in the sense of how you dress, how you where your hair, how you carry yourself and even how you speak. This change of image is not something forced or contrived, nor is it to do with keeping in step of fashion. It is likened to a snake shedding it's skin for new skin because it has outgrown the old. It is just something that has to happen because you now have a renewed mind.

A renewed mind will change the way you see yourself and you will no longer be able to go back to the person you were. This is because transfiguration is where YOU end and God begins! It is where purpose takes precedence over dreams and personal goals. Is it wrong to have dreams and personal goals? Not in the least! In the grand scheme of things dreams and goals serve as the carrot to lead you into your destiny.

Although he had to go to the pit before reaching the palace, Joseph's dream lead him to his divine destiny as savior to the nations. In his position as second only to the King of Egypt, he went from looking like a Hebrew to looking like an Egypt. His transfiguration was such that the Egyptians dined with him, although it was detestable for Egyptians to eat with Hebrews. Even his own brothers did not recognize him. Imagine the contrast from the modest appearance of a Hebrew to the elaborate decking of an Egyptian clad with costume jewellery, wigs and make up - and this was just the men!

Transfiguration is what is necessary to propel you through the glass ceiling, thus shattering it forever. A prime example of this is in the case of Barack Obama, who on January 20th 2009 became the first African-American president of the United States of America; forever shattering the seemingly impenetrable image of a US President. Although other black hopefuls had made an attempt for the Presidency, none matched the image, style, presence, character and message of change that exemplified Barak Obama. Transfiguration is what is necessary for you appeal to a greater and much wider audience. It is the difference between representing a community or particular culture, or representing a nation, country or even industry.

There is a word of warning that comes with transfiguration. Beauty is in the eye of the beholder and not everyone will like the new you! Although Joseph looked like someone who had sold his soul to Egypt, his heart was very much Hebrew. Unfortunately, many are quick to make judgement based on appearance rather than seeking insight. This is especially the case with those from whom you came from - your own brethren. However, like Joseph, you must realize that the Kingdom positions you in a place of influence ahead of time, that you may be a source of help to those who are behind.

When you are ahead of your time, misunderstanding is inevitable, however, as with the case of Esther, there is always a 'for such as time as this' moment to come, where your greatness will be needed, recognized and rewarded.

DISCOVERING YOUR HIDDEN TREASURE

The kingdom of heaven is like treasure hidden in a field. When a man found it, he hid it again, and then in his joy went and sold all he had and bought that field. Matthew 13:44 NIV.

Anything of great value that is hidden points to the subject of potential. The ability to recognize potential is key when it comes to making any sizeable investment. This is because potential is not always obvious and is only recognizable through knowledge of purpose, wisdom, insight and resources. Therefore it would be true to say that potential is in the eye of the beholder. Treasure

> TRUE POTENTIAL IS BASED ON WHAT GOD CAN DO THROUGH YOU

is not always something obvious like gold, jewels or money. I believe the treasure mentioned in the parable above, could have been found by any passer-by if they recognized it as treasure. Therefore the treasure was only hidden by the fact that it was not recognizable to the average passer-by.

One of my favorite TV shows is Dragons' Den, a venture capitalist TV program where budding entrepreneurs pitch their business ideas to five wealthy business people (the dragons), hoping to procure their required investment. Each dragon commands multi million pound enterprises and are amongst the most influential people in the UK. Once an entrepreneur (or contestant) has made their presentation, the dragons probe the validity of the idea often revealing an embarrassing lack of preparation on the part of the contestants. This often results in harsh, scathing opinions from the dragons.

Dragon's Den draws many parallels to the nature of God and His Kingdom. For instance, like the dragons, God is a willing investor:

THE EYES OF THE LORD SEARCH THE WHOLE EARTH IN ORDER TO STRENGTHEN THOSE WHOSE HEARTS ARE FULLY COMMITTED TO HIM (2 CHRONICLES 16:9 NLT)

God is searching for those in whom He can strengthen with the investment of His power. As long as you are willing to commit what you have to him, He is willing to commit what He has to you. This brings us to the key factors in discovering your hidden treasure. Having watched the show from its' inception, I have found that acquiring investment in the Dragon's Den was due to any of the following factors:

* the business idea was sound and scalable.

* the business idea could only work based on the specific resources of a particular dragon.

* the business idea was sound; however, the contestant recognized his/her own weakness in making it a success and were willing to allow the dragon(s) to have a greater stake (and control) of their business.

* the dragon had a better use for the product than what was proposed by the contestant.

* their business idea was weak; however, the contestant exuded personality and character that the dragons could work with.

These reasons parallel Kingdom principles for discovering and realizing your potential.

Integrity

Any good manufacturer has a quality control process to test the integrity (soundness) of its' product before releasing it in the market place. This is because an under performing or faulty product reflects badly on the manufacturer. In like manner, before God can release you in your specific field, you must pass the quality control test and show yourself approved.

BE DILIGENT TO PRESENT YOURSELF APPROVED TO GOD, A WORKER WHO DOES NOT NEED TO BE ASHAMED, RIGHTLY DIVIDING THE WORD OF TRUTH (2 TIMOTHY 2:15)

The word 'approved' is translated from the Greek word *dokimas*. This was the name given to honest money changers of the ancient world who would not accept counterfeit coins and only put genuine, full weighted money into circulation. They were given the name dokimas because they were men of integrity. A person of quality bears the hallmark of integrity.

Honesty is the outward show or manifestation of integrity, which stems from being whole, complete and undivided. The need to lie and deceive is the result of internal lack and brokenness. The building material to achieve wholeness is the Word of God (2 timothy 3:16). No matter what your gifting or purpose is, being grounded in God's Word is fundamental. Therefore we must study the Word and not just read it.

Excellence

In addition to the Word of God we must study pervasively and seek to become an expert in our field. God is a God of excellence and we too must adopt the spirit of excellence. When we seek excellence in all that we do we will become a workman that need not be ashamed.

Excellence demands that we develop the skills that would hone our talents.

THE LAZY MAN DOES NOT ROAST HIS GAME, BUT THE DILIGENT MAN PRIZES HIS POSSESSIONS (PROVERBS 12:27)

Talent is gift, but without skill it is just raw material. If you prize the talent you have, then you must be diligent in developing the necessary skills that would best utilize your talent. You may be a gifted singer, but can you perform? Do you have stamina? Do you have any business aptitude? Do you know how to speak to the media? These are just some of the skills you must develop in order to enhance your gift and achieve a successful career.

Scalability

You will only grow to the limits of your own beliefs. Therefore in order to be scalable it is vitally important to identify and eliminate self-limiting beliefs. To achieve this you must learn to rightly divide (handle with accuracy) the Word of truth (2 Timothy 2:15). Understanding the truth of God's Word will free you from all that hinders, especially self-limiting beliefs (John 8:32).

Ironically, the number one obstacle to understanding the truth of God's Word is religion. Religion is man's own remedy for dealing with the guilt of sin that gnaws at his soul. Anything rooted in guilt will only serve to bring condemnation, punishment and imprisonment, physically or mentally. That is why religious people (especially religious Christians) focus on what you cannot do. God desires for us to understand and live according to 'the law of the Spirit of Life in Christ Jesus' so that we can focus on what we can do (John 8:1-2).

It is imperative that you understand the difference between religious assumptions and the truth of God's Word. You will never realize the scale of your true potential if you don't. Embracing the truth of God's Word will cause you to be effective and marketable across multiple spectrums of people, cultures, genres, industries and a range of other divides. God has made us both Kings and Priest (Revelation 5:10). Therefore we have been endowed with the ability to be leaders in the marketplace as well as in the temple.

Divine Connections

Another key factor in the discovery of your potential is your ability to work with others. Purpose is never confined to one individual. God's will for your life is interlaced with the purpose and abilities of others. No matter how great your gift is, it's just a small part of God's master plan. Therefore your potential will only be released through divine connections. There are individuals who are ordained to be in your life whether for a season or for life. Recognizing these 'divine connections' and the role they are design to play in your life (and vice versa) is key to your success. So we will do well to remember that it takes teamwork to make the dream work.

Submission

You must be open to the fact that your hidden treasure may be the combination of your gifts and talents with the resources and wisdom of someone else. This may require you to submit under the authority of that person or allow them to have a greater say in what you do. Often times on Dragon's Den, it became apparent that one particular dragon was best suited in making a contestants idea work. However, it would also mean that the dragon required a larger stake in the company than what the contestant was willing to offer. It is at that point they were faced with the decision of either keeping 100% of nothing or 50% of millions.

No matter how capable you are, you are not designed to do it all by yourself. We all have strengths and weaknesses and it is important to know what they are. Just like a marriage, the strengths of one serves to compensate for the weakness of the other (and vice versa). That is the essence of covenant life.

Insight

Your purpose has larger implications than what you can presently see.

GOD HAS MADE EVERYTHING BEAUTIFUL FOR ITS OWN TIME. HE HAS PLANTED ETERNITY IN THE HUMAN HEART, BUT EVEN SO, PEOPLE CANNOT SEE THE WHOLE SCOPE OF GOD'S WORK FROM BEGINNING TO END (ECCLESIASTES 3:11 NLT)

There are people who see more in you than what you see in yourself. Dragon's Den contestants would often come under heavy criticism from the dragons because of their poor business ideas. Most of them would declare the contestant 'uninvestable.' However, there would be one dragon who usually keeps quiet while the others are raging. This is because he/she sees something that the others fail to see. When all the other dragons declare themselves 'out,' then they take cash-in and reveal to the others that the only thing preventing the contestant from being totally investable is a small 'tweak' in their business idea. Many of you only need a small adjustment in your attitude, focus, beliefs and ideas in order to experience outstanding success.

As mentioned, treasure is not always something that is obviously valuable. Your treasure is hidden from others because they only see your limitations. They themselves do not have the resources, insight and wisdom to utilize your abilities.

Wisdom

The wisdom of God is profoundly simple. That is why the most lucrative ideas are so simple you wonder why you did not think of it yourself. God deliberately chose things the world considers foolish in order to shame those who think they are wise (1 Corinthians 1:27).

Many who we call geniuses today were once considered *fools*. Therefore we must learn to trust in the wisdom of

God and not lean on our own understanding (Proverbs 3:5).

Character

In our opening parable, the man first found the treasure and then hid it again. Why didn't he just take the treasure? Often times we are not yet ready to be discovered. We may have the talent, skills and even the opportunity; but the one vital ingredient missing is character. Talent without character is a disaster waiting to happen. I once heard Joyce Meyers say, *"your talent can take you to heights your character cannot handle."* How many times have we watched on our screens with dismay, sorrow or delight the disgraceful behavior of gifted entertainers, athletes, politicians, ministers and the like. Many have reached the pinnacle of success only to be toppled by the revelation of their indiscretion. Indeed none of us are perfect, nor do we have to be perfect to be used of God. However, without character, fame and fortune will cause you to have a higher estimation of yourself than you ought. In your arrogance you will mistreat others and behave in a manner other than you would when you had nothing.

Character is not 'a given.' It is that which has to be developed and instilled over time. It is the product of trials, endurance and patience (Romans 5:3-4). Hence

God keeps us patiently hidden while we develop the character He is looking for. Like a master baker, He will only let us out of the oven when we are *fully cooked*. It is no surprise that the Greek word used for character is dokimas, the same word used for approved, as mentioned earlier. Character is God's seal of approval, not talent. God can do more with a person of little talent but good character, than with a person of great talent but poor character.

True potential is not about what you can do with your talent and abilities. It is based on what God can do through you. That is the treasure!

THE KINGDOM

KEYS TO KINGDOM PROMOTION

For the Kingdom of Heaven is as a man traveling into a far country, who called his own servants and delivered unto them his goods. And unto one he gave five talents, to another two and to another one; to every man according to his several (personal) ability; and straightway took his journey. Matthew 25:14-25 KJV.

In a time where job security is becoming a thing of the past and rumors abound that the world's most powerful countries are on the brink of recession, we can no longer rely on traditional means for financial security. Now more than ever, we need to press into the only thing that flourishes in the midst of war, terrorism and

> Knowledge is the currency of God's kingdom

economic decline; that is the Kingdom of Heaven. Jesus came to establish the Kingdom, (not a religion) and like all Kingdoms, the Kingdom of Heaven operates by principles or keys (Matthew 16:19). He used many parables to illustrate the Kingdom of Heaven and the principles by which it operates. The opening text introduces us to the 'Parable of the Talents'. In this parable I will highlight four key principles that guide us to promotion in the Kingdom.

Stewardship: God's Property

The servants in the parable are best described as stewards. A steward is someone who has the responsibility of managing someone else's property and affairs. Stewardship is a very important dynamic within God's Kingdom. As a steward you must resolve yourself to the fact that:

- you are not the owner of what you have

- you are accountable for what you have

- you are expected to take care of, improve and increase what you have as if it was your own.

This is the premise behind Kingdom thinking that must be adopted in order to live effectively in the kingdom. The power of stewardship lies in the relationship between the steward and the owner. The steward's responsibility is to manage what the owner has entrusted to him. The owners' responsibility is to ensure that the steward has everything necessary to carry out his responsibilities effectively. Jesus underlines this very fact when He said:

"Do not worry and be anxious, saying what shall we eat? Or what shall we drink? Or, what are we going to have to wear? For the gentiles wish for and diligently seek these things, and your heavenly Father knows you need them all. But seek first the Kingdom and His righteousness and all these things shall be added to you" (Matthew 6:31-33)

Many believers miss out on God's provision due to the issue of ownership. God is not responsible for what you own. He is responsible for what He owns. You may argue that God owns everything as quoted in Psalms 24:1 and therefore He is responsible for our provision; and indeed you are right. However there is a difference between provision for existence and provision for living. Jesus came that we might have life in abundance (John 10:10). Therefore the provision that is required is that which pertains to the abundant life. Kingdom life is not about having the bare necessities; it is about being a giver. It is hard to give (cheerfully) when what you have is what you need! We must understand that we are God's property (1 Corinthians 6:20). When we live by our own agenda and refuse to relinquish ownership of our lives to God, we deactivate the principles for provision in our lives; but when the objectives of the King and His kingdom become our first priority, we attract into our lives everything we need and more.

Righteousness: God's Standard

Righteousness can be defined as God's way of doing things. It is the principle or STANDARD by which everything is judged. Righteousness is God's stamp of approval. What is God's standard? What are His expectations? According to the parable, the master gave his stewards a number of talents according to their personal ability. When he returned after a long journey, he expected to see increase of his wealth. Increase is the evidence of righteousness. God is a God of excellence. That being the case, when we do things according to God's way we will excel. To excel is to increase, and increase is the result of productivity. God judges things by how productive they are. Jesus said:

"I AM THE TRUE VINE AND MY FATHER IS THE VINE DRESSER. ANY BRANCH IN ME THAT DOES NOT BEAR FRUIT HE CUTS AWAY; AND HE CLEANSES AND REPEATEDLY PRUNES EVERY BRANCH THAT CONTINUES TO BEAR FRUIT, TO MAKE IT BEAR MORE AND RICHER AND MORE EXCELLENT FRUIT" (JOHN 15:1-2)

It is important to note that in Christ, righteousness has been conferred upon us. However this is more than a title; this is assurance that we can be and should be productive.

Excellence - Personal Development

What was the determining factor in how much each servant should receive? According to the parable each servant received talents based on their personal ability. The master knew the capabilities of his servants and this was reflected in the amount of responsibility he gave each of them. It suggests that this was not the first time the stewards had been tested in this way, probably with smaller things. Your spiritual (greater) ambitions will only be realized when you have proved yourself faithful in that which pertains to every day living.

We all have the potential to be great. That potential will only be realized when we make a commitment to our own personal development. As a believer, what you achieve in life is the result of your supernatural partnership with God. God enhances your natural abilities with His super abilities; so if you do nothing, you achieve nothing. Laziness is a big NO-NO in the Kingdom! This is where the one talent steward got it so wrong. As a steward, not only was his attitude wrong regarding the master's right to the fruit of his labor

*THE KINGDOM

(Matthew 25:24), but also he did nothing with his talent except bury it.

The Apostle Paul urges us to be *'transformed by the renewing of our minds'* (Romans 12:2). Renewing your mind is not a one-time event. It is a perpetual cycle of improving the quality of your mind. Knowledge is the currency of the kingdom of God, therefore the more you learn the more you can acquire. This is why the five-talent steward knew what to do with the talents straight away. He had invested his time wisely in improving his mind. This state of perpetual improvement can be summed up in one word – Excellence! God is a God of Excellence and we too must adopt a spirit of excellence.

Leadership - The Acid Test

All of the stages mentioned find their purpose in leadership. Leadership is when you come into your own. It is the accumulation of your stewardship, knowing God's will, your ability to be fruitful and your commitment to excellence. The master going on a long journey is indicative of God taking a step back to see what you are really made of. This is the acid test of your ability to put what He has taught you into action. What do you do when God seems distant; when the answers to your prayers do not come so readily? Proverbs 4:7 states; *"get wisdom and with your getting, get understanding."*

The purpose of you getting wisdom is to enable you to make wise and godly decisions. Religious Christianity teaches us to be totally dependant upon God. Unfortunately this is often taken to the extreme where we become disempowered through our expectation of God to sort everything out for us.

In contrast, the five-talent steward knew exactly what to do when his master left. He immediately went and traded with them and gained five talents more. There was no need to spend more time seeking God's will again because he already knew what it was. Once you are fully prepared all that is left is to recognize and seize opportunities.

In conclusion, we live on levels and arrive there in stages. These keys are steps that God has designed to elevate us from one level to the next. It is His will for you to live in the abundance of Kingdom life and enjoy the blessedness He enjoys. To be entrusted with the affairs of God's Kingdom and the wealth that comes with it, personal leadership is the quality most required.

*THE KINGDOM

A CALL TO REPENTANCE

Repent for the Kingdom of God is at hand! (Matthew 4:17)

For many, hearing the word 'repentance' evokes thoughts of someone running to the church altar and sorrowfully crying out to God for forgiveness. For some it is vowing not to do a particular sin and doing all you can to curb your behavior and resist temptation. However, careful study of the original Greek text points to a particular kind of repentance which does not call for the reactions mentioned.

#THE KINGDOM

> IMPROVING YOUR LIFE STARTS WITH IMPROVING THE QUALITY OF YOUR THOUGHTS

You may be surprised to know that in the original (Greek) language the new testament was written in, the word Jesus used for repentance has nothing to do with seeking for forgiveness or feeling regret due of the consequences of one's actions. Instead it means to 'change your mind' as a result of knowledge received. Thus Jesus' call to repentance is a call to embrace a new way of thinking in order to function effectively in the Kingdom. Everything that Jesus did and taught after that was to communicate the Kingdom-thinking He wants us to now embrace. Jesus said:

"AND NO ONE PUTS NEW WINE INTO OLD WINESKINS. THE OLD SKINS WOULD BURST FROM THE PRESSURE, SPILLING THE WINE AND RUINING THE SKINS. NEW WINE MUST BE STORED IN NEW WINESKINS. THAT WAY BOTH THE WINE AND THE WINESKINS ARE PRESERVED" (MATTHEW 9:17 NLT)

Likewise, you will never receive the benefits of the Kingdom without a significant change to how you think. Restraining behavior without changing the thoughts that fuel them, is like trying to hold a beach ball under water. Eventually the behavior will surface 'when' you take your hands off the ball.

How you think is key to all that you will experience in life because your reality is the product of *thoughts*. Ignorance of this very fact causes many to ask or pray for things that their reality simply does not support. Thus, like the old wineskins, they are incapable of receiving or maintaining the blessings they so much desire.

The parable of the talents (Matthew 25:14-30) shows us that you can give a man $5000 and he can double it over time. You can give another man (in similar circumstances) $1000 and he will end up losing it and more. I would venture to say the same outcome may occur if they were both given either $5000 or $1000. Both men shared similar circumstances; but according to the parable, the steward who lost it all, did so as a result of the ill thoughts he harbored against the master - colloquially called 'stinking thinking.' To quote James Allen (author of 'As a Man Thinketh):

"MEN ARE ANXIOUS TO IMPROVE THEIR CIRCUMSTANCES, BUT ARE UNWILLING TO IMPROVE THEMSELVES, THEY THEREFORE REMAIN BOUND."

Improving your life starts with improving the quality of your thoughts. Hence Paul teaches that transformation takes place through the qualitative renewing of the mind (Romans 12:2). The quality of your life is a direct reflection of the quality of your thoughts. The key to effective living can be found in this one sentence:

✦THE KINGDOM

"SEEK FIRST THE KINGDOM OF GOD AND HIS RIGHTEOUSNESS AND ALL THESE THINGS SHALL BE ADDED UNTO YOU" (MATTHEW 6:33 KJV)

Simply put, seeking the Kingdom of God and His righteousness involves learning how to think like God. That is why belief is so key in Jesus' teachings. What you believe determines what you will receive. Hence to the 'believer', God gives His Spirit so that he or she may have His mind - the mind of Christ:

BUT GOD HAS REVEALED THEM TO US THROUGH HIS SPIRIT. FOR THE SPIRIT SEARCHES ALL THINGS, YES, THE DEEP THINGS OF GOD. FOR WHAT MAN KNOWS THE THINGS OF A MAN EXCEPT THE SPIRIT OF THE MAN WHICH IS IN HIM? EVEN SO NO ONE KNOWS THE THINGS OF GOD EXCEPT THE SPIRIT OF GOD. NOW WE HAVE RECEIVED, NOT THE SPIRIT OF THE WORLD, BUT THE SPIRIT WHO IS FROM GOD, THAT WE MIGHT KNOW THE THINGS THAT HAVE BEEN FREELY GIVEN TO US BY GOD. THESE THINGS WE ALSO SPEAK, NOT IN WORDS WHICH MAN'S WISDOM TEACHES BUT WHICH THE HOLY SPIRIT TEACHES, COMPARING SPIRITUAL THINGS WITH SPIRITUAL. BUT THE NATURAL MAN DOES NOT RECEIVE THE THINGS OF THE SPIRIT OF GOD, FOR THEY ARE FOOLISHNESS TO HIM; NOR CAN HE KNOW THEM, BECAUSE THEY ARE SPIRITUALLY DISCERNED. BUT HE WHO IS SPIRITUAL JUDGES ALL THINGS, YET HE HIMSELF IS RIGHTLY JUDGED BY NO ONE. FOR "WHO HAS KNOWN THE MIND OF THE LORD THAT HE MAY INSTRUCT HIM?" BUT WE HAVE THE MIND OF CHRIST (1 CORINTHIANS 2:10-16)

Thinking like God grants us access to the endless resources of the Kingdom, enabling us to attract into our lives whatever we need or desire. If we want to experience the promise of God's abundance we must embrace His thoughts pertaining to that promise.

Your mind is the center of your life and thus the place where we must allow God to occupy. Due to the magnetizing power of your mind, you cannot afford to let fear, doubt or discouragement have a stronghold in your mind, otherwise you will attract into your life that which you most fear. You must guard your mind at all costs! Hence Paul states:

"DO NOT BE ANXIOUS ABOUT ANYTHING, BUT IN EVERYTHING, BY PRAYER AND PETITION, WITH THANKSGIVING, PRESENT YOUR REQUESTS TO GOD. AND THE PEACE OF GOD, WHICH TRANSCENDS ALL UNDERSTANDING, WILL GUARD YOUR HEARTS AND YOUR MINDS IN CHRIST JESUS" (PHILIPIANS 4:6-7 NKJV).

Notice the text does not say that God will give you what you requested. Instead God will guard your mind with His peace. This is because that which you want has to be manifested through your mind. Having His peace guarding your mind will grant you the protection and the focus you need to bring about what you desire.

With His peace you are now able to develop the quality of your thoughts and embrace kingdom thinking:

THE KINGDOM

"Finally, brothers, whatever is true, whatever is noble, whatever is right, whatever is pure, whatever is lovely, whatever is admirable - if anything is excellent or praiseworthy think about such things" (Philipians 4:8 NIV)

PERSONAL POWER

✤PERSONAL POWER

A WINNING PERSPECTIVE

The very fact that you have lawsuits among you means you have been completely defeated already. Why not rather be wronged? Why not rather be cheated?
1 Corinthians 6:7

A dear friend of mine sought my advice regarding an issue her 17 year old son was facing. He attended a prominent youth academy which placed him at a company to gain work experience (on a non-salaried basis). He worked as a graphic designer, creating some of the publicity needed for the firm's marketing campaigns and events.

> **NEVER LET OFFENCE CLOUD YOUR JUDGEMENT**

A year after his tenure at the academy he was approached by the director of that company and asked if he would design a logo and a brochure. Apart from a promissory gesture by the director to introduce him to his contacts, no payment was offered. The teenager gladly did the work; but things soon became sour when the director became evasive every time the subject of introducing him to his contacts was raised. At the same time he put the boy under scathing pressure to complete the work to a tight deadline.

His mother was understandably concerned that her son was being taken advantage of and prepared a 'well crafted' letter to send to the director. However, mindful not to jeopardise potential opportunities for her son, she decided to seek my advice before sending it, due to my years of experience in the creative industry. As she described the case to me I was able to confirm that her son was indeed being taken advantage of. This company usually pays for designers to do their work and the director was using her son to avoid the expense of design fees. She had every right to be upset at how her son was being treated and the company director was deserving of a good 'ticking' off. However, I was still apprehensive about her sending the letter (yet) as I too shared her initial concerns about jeopardizing his future.

No matter how diplomatic or well crafted her letter was, the fact that it was coming from his mother (seen to be the lioness) could've resulted in the director distancing himself and his company from her son and any possible trouble associated with him. Instead I decided to look at the situation from a different perspective and sought to give another meaning to this situation.

Her son was just starting out in his career and oftentimes designers work on a freelance basis where the ability to sell oneself is key. I saw this situation as a golden opportunity for her son to gain some business acumen and negotiate with the director. From the caliber of work her son was commissioned to do, it became obvious that the director had confidence in his abilities and talent. This would serve as leverage for her son to demand design credits (if payment was not forthcoming) for the ongoing tasks and to negotiate suitable payment for future jobs. If the director disagreed, then a letter of complaint was due.

She passed on my advice to her son who acted accordingly. Two weeks later I was delighted to hear that he was successful in obtaining what he asked for, birthing the beginning of business relationship with the company.

Opportunities do not always come in attractive packages. The picture that adversity paints is not necessarily as gloomy as it seems. You posses the ability to look at the imagery of dire circumstances and frame it with a meaning that empowers you. No circumstance is set in stone and it's impact on you is subject only to the definition you give to it. There are situations beyond our control; but the meaning we give to them is key, as it is responsible for how we feel about it. How we feel determines our actions, and all actions have a consequence. Therefore, meaning controls outcome! The good thing is that you can choose or even create the meaning you want to give to any circumstance you face. Debt problems can serve as a lesson in financial management. Divorce can serve as a powerful medium for re-evaluation and self discovery. No matter how ugly the situation, its impact on you is subject only to the meaning you give to it.

Your mind will always seek to find a meaning to any given situation. Unfortunately, by default, the mind leans toward pessimism, hence the initial tendency of thinking the worst in any given situation. We must make a conscious effort to train our minds to think on things that will empower rather than discourage us. A well trained mind that seeks to find the good in any given situation is a mind that can steer you to a life of success.

The most powerful way of training your mind to explore and find meanings that will empower you is to see things from a 'winning' perspective. A winning perspective is where you see yourself in a position where you have the advantage. It is where you see yourself as the head and not the tail, above and not beneath. When you see yourself as always having the advantage, your only dilemma is deciding how you want to win.

In the opening text, Paul rebukes believers for the act of taking each other to court and poses a notion that many of us will have trouble agreeing with:

WHY NOT RATHER BE WRONGED? WHY NOT RATHER BE CHEATED?

Understandably, no one wants to be cheated or wronged. Many of us are quick to fight if we feel slighted in anyway. However, we must be mindful that in the midst of fighting over the little that was lost, we do not end up loosing the greater that could have been gained. When Paul posed that question, he was looking at things from a heavenly perspective. From Heaven's viewpoint those who are appointed to judge and govern the world disqualify themselves when they show that they cannot resolve comparatively trivial matters between themselves. From that point of view it would be better to allow yourself to be wronged in such matters than to loose your inheritance as a world ruler.

In conclusion, never let an offence cloud your judgment. Always keep your eye on the big picture and the end goal. When faced with situations that seek to disempower you, look for or create an alternative meaning that puts power back in your hands. When you do this, a raft of opportunities will be revealed to you that you would not have otherwise seen.

BREAKING MENTAL BARRIERS

The way of the lazy man is like a hedge of thorns, But the way of the upright is a highway. Proverbs 15:19

When we speak of mental barriers, we are talking about a train of thought or belief that prevents us from carrying out activities we know we need to complete. The symptom of this is procrastination. Procrastination, in layman's terms, is putting off something for tomorrow that was meant to be done *last year*. It is the soil that makes difficulties grow. Procrastination give rise to

> CLARITY IS REALLY
> ABOUT MAKING
> THINGS SIMPLE

laziness, both bearing the same consequences, namely missed opportunities and poor results. The bible expresses strong views about laziness and none of it is complimentary. Laziness is not just a matter of having a poor work ethic. You can be hard-working in one area of your life and sluggish in another. However, handwork sometimes serves as a distraction or substitute from doing the things in your life which you know are more important. Activities that bring short-lived gratification smother important tasks. How many times have you set out to accomplish a relevant task but were distracted along the way, which either led to the job not being done in time or not at all? Do you find it difficult to remain focused on a particular assignment and seeing it through to the end? Like an alcoholic who must first admit he is an alcoholic in order to gain help, we too must identify the areas in our lives which have suffered from neglect, and own up to our laziness.

In the opening text, a hedge of thorns was used as a fence to surround a vineyard. An encounter with thorns is usually a painful one. In like manner to the hedge of thorns the mind of the lazy is fenced in by mental barriers. These barriers come to light when particular activities have an association with a mental form of pain; or better yet perceived pain. We have a perception that a particular activity will be difficult or uncomfortable or even costly. For example many business owners or self-employed workers hate administrative work (myself included). The thought of doing it brings about the perception of pain and they would rather be doing the activity they are passionate about. Another example is in physical exercise. How many times have you given up in the middle (or near the end) of a particular exercise, not because of physical limitation but mental. In both cases there is strong association with pain, which prevents you from starting something or even continuing, and ultimately you do not achieve the results you desire. Hence the proverb:

"THE APPETITE OF THE SLUGGARD CRAVES AND GETS NOTHING, BUT THE APPETITE OF THE DILIGENT IS ABUNDANTLY SUPPLIED" (PROVERBS 13:4 AMPLIFIED).

Mental barriers are like veils that cover the mind and obscure the truth about our true potential. If we do not learn to break these barriers we will remain trapped by our own self imposed limitations. Mental barriers can be overcome by first understanding the reasons for this perception of pain. This pain is the result of insecurities harbored in the mind. Because of the many insecurities we have as humans, safety in all aspects of life is an important need. We all tend to have comfort zones that we like to live in, whether it be in our career, social life, finances or even spiritually. There is a certain limit that we would not go pass, or a certain amount of risk we are not willing to take. An example of this can be found in seeking the approval of our peers. Not many of us are willing to stand out or go against the grain because of the fear of failure. Like sheep, many of us prefer to follow rather than lead.

Conflicts emerge when change challenges what we are comfortable with. The arrival of change brings about insecurity and the perception of pain. Change could be going to the gym, changing your diet, learning to use the Internet, reading more, even socializing; the list is endless but you know what applies to you. Change demands for us to extend the boundaries of our comfort zone or to come out of it altogether. Although change is not always welcome, it is necessary for growth, development and maturity to take place. This is why we only embrace change when it is absolutely necessary or when the consequence of not doing so leaves us in a place of insecurity.

This conflict between change and our misplaced securities produces the cement that keeps mental barriers in place; namely excuses based on perceived fears.

THE SLUGGARD SAYS THERE IS A LION OUTSIDE, I SHALL BE SLAIN! (PROVERBS 22:13)

Is there a lion in the street, or is it really just a domestic cat. If we do not test the validity of our excuses, we give room for goals to appear less achievable.

The key stage in breaking mental barriers is analyzing self-limiting beliefs. Belief is the foundation of our attitude and our actions. Our beliefs rest upon what we conclude as evidence. Our belief is only as strong as the evidence that supports it. Self-limiting beliefs rest on evidence formed through fear. If we examine the validity of these beliefs, we will find that a great deal of logic and common sense has been overlooked in order to form these conclusions.

What do you believe is holding you back? There are two types of belief, ones that are helpful and others that are not. We would do well to identify the beliefs that are not helpful and then ask this question: what else has to be true for this to be true? For example you may blame your ethnicity for not being able to move ahead. For that to be true you will also have to believe that every body else of your ethnicity cannot move ahead. You conclude that you cannot loose weight because obesity is a disease. For that to be true you will have to believe that no one else with the same disease can be cured.

Many people create all manner of justifications and rationalizations for poor performance. They convince themselves that they lack the potential and ability of other people who are successful, based upon the flimsiest of evidence. The real tragedy is that most people sell themselves short by settling for far less than what they are truly capable of becoming. In reality we all have similar mental ability and potential. Everyone has the same brain structure. Everyone has a variety of talents and abilities. We all have the same amount of muscles. The only difference between Mr Universe and the average person is that he has invested the time and the effort in developing his muscles. Some people start off with greater natural advantages and personal endowments, but on average, each of us has the ability to develop far beyond anything we have achieved so far. The only real limits on what you can do or be are the limits you accept in your own mind.

Thus we need to change the way we see ourselves. Sight is the faculty of the mind and not the eyes. To put it another way, we see with our mind and not our eyes. It is your mind that gives meaning to the streams of light and colors that pass through your eyes. Your eyes are merely a window that gives one dimension of sight to your mind. Therefore seeing yourself differently requires you to redefine yourself in order to change your perception of yourself. To redefine yourself you must believe in a better you, using faith as your intangible but very real evidence to support your belief.

As stated before, many of us derive our self-image from the meaning we give to our experiences in life. God sees us in an entirely different light despite our experiences. We are high powered (a royal people), highly intelligent (with the mind of Christ), highly influential (favored), highly valued (blood bought) highly skilled (anointed) and highly paid (blessed). You are God's masterpiece!

The Need for Clarity

Another consideration for breaking mental barriers is the need for clarity. We need clear values, clear goals, clear vision (destiny), clear roles and a clear self image. Clarity will enable you to stay focused even when chaos reigns all around you. Decisions are easier to make when you have clarity. The (mental) law of concentration postulates that the more you focus and concentrate on your goals, the quicker your goals will be achieved. Your ability to concentrate on your goals is dependent on the clarity of your goals (and the passion you have to achieve them).

Confusion is the presence of things that are of no help to you. This is true of your external circumstances as well as your internal thoughts and beliefs. Therefore clarity can be obtained by identifying what helps you and what hinders you and eliminating the latter. What thoughts are hindering you? What beliefs are hindering you? What habits are hindering you? WHO is hindering you? When looking at who is hindering you, it is important to distinguish between those who should not be in your life and those who are purposely placed in your life to present challenges. Don't avoid challenges as they present the opportunity for promotion.

Clarity is really about making things simple. The mental barriers that stand in our way are the result of a confused and cluttered mind. Cluttered with beliefs that only serve to limit and devalue us. We do not realize how much mental energy is being spent by the needless processing of triviality within the mind. All action starts from mental energy or thought impulse. When this energy is wasted on things of no benefit, we find it difficult to become motivated. This is energy that could be better used in more creative endeavors that make the difference between broke and millionaire status.

One of the most effective tools for making room in your mind is the *wastepaper basket*. You will be surprised at the difference it will make to your mind by throwing out all the junk mail, magazines, post-it notes etc. that have been stored for weeks, months or even years. Each of those things holds a place in your mind as something you have to deal with at some later date. The fact that you have not dealt with it by now is proof that it cannot be that important. Try it for yourself, go through your office or entire house and have a good clear out. Be brutal and resist the urge to hoard. You will notice the difference to your mind immediately.

To gain clarity you become organized. The mantra for being organized is 'a place for everything and everything in its place'. A disorganized person uses more physical and mental energy just to function than someone who is organized. When you are organized you can operate with greater speed and efficiency. I cannot stress the importance of being organized. Being disorganized is the main reason for failure in all aspects of life. Therefore it is vital to get into the habit of organizing your life.

To be highly effective at this you must have a clear vision of your mission in life. What are you passionate about? Passion is love and anger combined. Martin Luther King was angry about racism. Mother Teresa was angry about poverty and destitution. Are you willing to move from complaining about life's issues to actually doing something about it? God has made each of us unique. I believe that in our uniqueness lies the solution for a particular problem. Success is measured by your ability to solve problems.

It is important to write a mission statement as stipulated in Habakkuk 2:2. Writing down your mission has the effect of crystallizing or engraving your goal in your mind. Your mind is the rudder of your life causing you to move in the direction of your most dominant thoughts. Get into the habit of reading, analyzing and rewriting your mission. By doing this you will develop more clarity as you start to understand the breadth and depth of what your mission entails. For example, when I started my graphic design business (Ministry In Art), my slogan was 'communicating vision in graphic excellence'. As the years passed, I developed a wider sense of my purpose and realized that this slogan was too restrictive as it pertained only to graphic design. I have a deep passion to see people excel in life and have dedicated much of my time in studying the art of achievement and human potential. This is for the sole purpose of teaching others through various mediums of communication. Now Ministry In Art has evolved into a media company with the slogan 'Communicating Excellence'. Less words, greater scope!

Once you are clear about your purpose, you must make choices that are congruent with that purpose. This is the key element to organizing your life. Remember this three pronged rule:

'life management = time management = decision management'

The outcome of your life is determined entirely upon the quality of your decisions. God declares in Deuteronomy 30:19:

"I HAVE SET BEFORE YOU LIFE AND DEATH, THE BLESSINGS AND

THE CURSES; THEREFORE CHOOSE LIFE, THAT YOU AND YOUR DESCENDANTS MAY LIVE."

Life can be defined as purpose, as this is the only reason for your existence. Therefore death is any option contrary to your purpose. All decisions boiled down to life and death! It is important to note that the scripture says, "that you and your descendants may live." Purpose related decisions pertain to all aspects of life especially your family and choice of spouse. The different areas of your life are all intricately linked. A bad decision in your social life can have drastic effects on your family or career.

Structuring your life in this way you will develop an acute sense of focus, which is the objective of having clarity. When focus is absent, confusion reigns. Focus is powerful and will help you to overcome every hurdle and to endure the test of time. Focus enables you to see through the walls of your present circumstances. When you have focus, mental barriers crumble.

*PERSONAL POWER

THE POWER OF FOCUS

For our light affliction, which is but for a moment, is working for us a far more exceeding and eternal weight of glory, while we do not look at the things which are seen, but at the things which are not seen. For the things which are seen are temporary, but the things which are not seen are eternal. 2 Corinthians 4:17-18

The writer, (Paul) presents a seemingly nonchalant attitude towards affliction. As painful as the experience may be, Paul describes it as a 'light' affliction. We might be tempted to think that Paul could not relate to the challenges that we are going through; but in fact he suffered greatly in order to preach the gospel. He was

✦PERSONAL POWER

FOCUS DETERMINES
YOUR DIRECTION IN LIFE

beaten, stoned, whipped, shipwrecked, imprisoned, persecuted, endured long periods of hunger, thirst and destitution. How is it that he was able to carry out his mandate with unfettered determination in the face of such hardship and pain?
With reference to our opening text, our afflictions only become lighter as we become weightier. In other words, when we choose to stand in the midst of pain, a transformation or growth takes place, which gives us the strength of character to best handle it. Like someone who regularly works out in the gym with weights, the more resistance you work with, the stronger you become. As you become stronger, weights that you struggled with in the past seem comparatively lighter. You then become able to exercise with more challenging weights.

Just as the objective of physical exercise is to develop certain muscles, life presents challenges that will potentially develop and bring about certain qualities in us that would not have come to light any other way. It is astounding to hear of people who have been through the most traumatic of experiences, yet manage to somehow turn a horrific experience into something positive and empowering. Although they fell apart at first, they managed to pick up the shattered pieces of their lives and go on to do remarkable things.

Going through bad experiences is not the key to bringing out the greatness within, just as lifting weights is not the key to becoming stronger. For every one person who has triumphed over adversity, there are dozens, even hundreds more that have fallen, never to rise again. So what is the key determining factor between success and failure, victory and defeat? Paul gives us the answer:

"W̲ʜɪʟᴇ ᴡᴇ ʟᴏᴏᴋ ɴᴏᴛ ᴀᴛ ᴛʜᴇ ᴛʜɪɴɢs ᴡʜɪᴄʜ ᴀʀᴇ sᴇᴇɴ, ʙᴜᴛ ᴀᴛ ᴛʜᴇ ᴛʜɪɴɢs ᴡʜɪᴄʜ ᴀʀᴇ ɴᴏᴛ sᴇᴇɴ..." (2 Cᴏʀɪɴᴛʜɪᴀɴs 4:18)

Notice he says "while." In other words, affliction only works to develop our character while we are doing something in the meantime. That something centers on what you choose to focus on. Focus is the key determining factor between success and failure. Focus determines your direction in life. You cannot ride a bike straight ahead whilst looking to the left; you will inevitably begin to veer to the left. In like manner, your life will veer towards what your mind is focused on.

Focus cultivates the indispensable quality of self discipline, described by Napoleon Hill as "The master key to riches." Goals cannot be achieved without focus. Focus enables you to keep at it, even when you cannot see immediate results. When you concentrate on a goal, never taking your eyes off it, you are guaranteed to reach that goal.

No one can steal your gift, talent or ability, but if your focus is broken, then your gift and talent will be of non-effect. It is important to know that staying focused is not just about avoiding distractions. What you focus on can be just as detrimental as being totally distracted from what you want to achieve. Many of us have fallen prey to the tendency of majoring on minors; in other words focusing on things that in the scheme of things are unimportant and unhelpful.

"Your ability to divert your attention from activities of a lower value to activities of higher value is central to everything you accomplish in life" - Brian Tracy.

It is important to practice this in every area of your life, especially in relationships where there is a tendency for 'everything' to become an important issue. Learn to define and prioritize what is important to you in a pyramid structure. Higher value priorities can only be 'few' towards the top of your pyramid and only 'one' thing of great importance can fit on the very top.

The Power of Vision

In the midst of trying times there is a natural inclination to look at your immediate circumstances and feel sorry for yourself. This may lead to worry, anxiety or even depression. Paul tells us not to look at things which are seen, but at the things which are not seen. This may seem quite strange; how can you look at something not seen? However, Paul is guiding us to where our focus should be. Not on our visible situation but on things that do exist although they are yet unseen.

There are multiple applications to employing this principle, having a clear vision is one of them. Vision is the picture of a compelling future. Not everyone will be able to see your vision, even if you explain it to them; so it is important that you see it and never take your eyes off it.

There is a law in psychology that if you form a picture in your mind of what you would like to be and you keep and hold that picture long enough, you will soon become exactly as you have been thinking. That is why God brought Abraham outside of his tent and said:

"Look now towards the heavens and count the stars - if you are able to number them. So shall your descendants be" (Genesis 15:5)

I believe this mental picture was the unseen force that enabled him to become the father of faith. This vision of the stars enabled him to believe in hope against hope that he might become the father of many nations. It was vision that caused him not to 'stagger at the promises of God' or to consider his body impotent even though he was about one hundred years old. Even the barrenness of his wife's womb was not considered an obstacle to giving birth to the promised seed (Romans 4:17-20).

Now faith is the substance of things hoped for, the evidence of things not seen (Hebrews 11:1)

Vision is the prerequisite to faith. This is because faith in essence is an act based on what you hope for and hope is based on what you see. When you see someone acting on faith, you are witnessing evidence of a vision known to them but yet to be revealed to everyone else.

Vision equates to hope and hope stimulates the mind, causing it to be more resourceful in the midst of a crisis. Hope brings you peace of mind when all others are loosing theirs. Your actions, aspirations, plans and beliefs all rest on the table of hope. With so much at stake, it is essential that your table of hope has strong legs. If they collapse, your whole life is lost! That is why Paul urges us not to focus on things seen because they are only temporal, whereas things unseen are eternal. In other words you cannot keep your focus (or rely) on what you can see, because it is temporal.

During times of crisis the best place to hang out is in your *future*. This is not escapism (in a negative sense), but the very means of bringing you through the situation. No matter how far fetched your vision seems, continue to entertain and embrace it.

The Principle of seeing The Unseen

Everything that can be seen is a manifestation of things unseen. Things seen are rooted in things unseen. Solutions are only found in things unseen. Things unseen are more real than things seen. These are some of the most important truths you can learn in life. Once you embrace these as a principle, they will change the way you respond to any given situation.

The Law of Recognition

The principle of seeing the unseen is not confined to a comparison between the tangible and the intangible. Things seen and unseen also refer to things noticed or things unnoticed. One of the fundamental keys to achievement in any area of life comes from your ability to recognize opportunities. God planted Adam in the Garden of Eden, an environment filled with food, water, gold, bdellium, onyx and other natural resources. We too are planted in our own Garden of Eden, filled with precious resources waiting to be recognized and unearthed.

By the principle of recognition you are able to see

opportunities and solutions that nobody else around you can see. One person while walking in the woods may see a flower and walk pass it because they perceive it to be just another flower. Another person may come across the same flower, carefully unearth it and carry it to the horticultural authorities, having just discovered one of the world's rarest varieties of flower. Sadly, everyday many are overlooking the people, resources and opportunities that are there to help them.

Your ability to recognize opportunities is enhanced when you are focused on a set goal. There is a saying *"When the student is ready, the teacher appears."* When you make a firm decision to accomplish a goal, and ultimately your vision, things start to happen to aid you on your journey. Some people will come into your life, some will exit. Unexpected situations occur, some pleasant and some unpleasant. These things may seem confusing at first, but if you remain focused you will begin to recognize that all of these things are working together for your good (Romans 8:28).

Furthermore, when you take steps to upgrade your personal knowledge (and skills) pertaining to your goals, you are guaranteed to recognize hidden opportunities. Knowledge made the difference between the man who failed to recognize the flower and the one who did? What you know determines what you see. What you can see is essential to transforming your world.

Final Thoughts...

You are the product of the choices you make in your environment. Don't abort your future by making rash decisions based on your present circumstances. It is by no coincidence that words serve only as a label for image they carry. Image is a very powerful commodity and you must speak words that carry images conducive with the vision you have for your life.

✤PERSONAL POWER

THE POWER OF CHOICE

"Today I have given you the choice between life and death, between blessings and curses. I call on heaven and earth to witness the choice you make. Oh, that you would choose life, that you and your descendants might live!" Deuteronomy 30:19 NLT

In life we experience all kinds of pressures that want to squeeze us into a particular mold to suit someone other than ourselves. This can come from society, your family, your peers, your place of employment or even your spouse. In a world with such pressures how can we be true to ourselves?

♦PERSONAL POWER

ERADICATE EVERY EXCUSE FOR NOT ACHIEVING YOUR GOALS

The first thing you must realize is that nobody can make you do what you do not want to do. Even in the most dire of situations where there seems to be no choice, you always have the power to choose how you want to respond. Many have come to the conclusion that we are the product of our environment, our society or even our genetic code. But the truth is we are the product of our chosen response to our environment, society and any situation that we have encountered. For many this statement may seem very condemning, especially if they blame society, racism, injustice, poverty, family breakdown or other bad experiences for their shortcomings. Although these things have a powerful impact upon us, nothing can rob us of choice. In other words we cannot control (to an extent) the unexpected things that happen to us, but we can control how we respond to them.

Choice has given us the power of self control. An extreme and moving example of this can be found in Victor Frankl's book 'Man's Search for Meaning.' This book is about Frankl's experience in a concentration camp, a place designed for both physical and mental torture. Frankl wrote:

"...EVERYTHING CAN BE TAKEN AWAY FROM A MAN BUT ONE THING: THE LAST OF HUMAN FREEDOM – TO CHOOSE ONE'S ATTITUDE IN ANY

GIVEN SET OF CIRCUMSTANCES, TO CHOOSE ONE'S WAY. THE WAY IN WHICH A MAN ACCEPTS HIS FATE AND ALL THE SUFFERING IT ENTAILS, THE WAY IN WHICH HE TAKES UP HIS CROSS, GIVES HIM AMPLE OPPORTUNITY – EVEN IN THE MOST DIFFICULT CIRCUMSTANCES – TO ADD A DEEPER MEANING TO HIS LIFE."

Frankl was able to create a positive experience out of what life had handed out to him.

Jesus underlined the principle of self control when he said:

"YOU HAVE HEARD THAT IT WAS SAID, AN EYE FOR AN EYE, AND A TOOTH FOR A TOOTH. BUT I SAY TO YOU, DO NOT RESIST THE EVIL MAN; BUT IF ANYONE STRIKES YOU ON THE RIGHT CHEEK, TURN TO HIM THE OTHER ONE TOO. AND IF ANYONE WANTS TO SUE YOU AND TAKE YOUR TUNIC, LET HIM HAVE YOUR COAT ALSO. AND IF ANYONE FORCES YOU TO GO ONE MILE, GO WITH HIM TWO. LOVE YOUR ENEMIES AND PRAY FOR THOSE WHO PERSECUTE YOU, TO SHOW THAT YOU ARE THE CHILDREN OF YOUR FATHER WHO IS IN HEAVEN" (MATTHEW 5:38 – 41 AND 44-45)

These examples are an indicator of the power of choice each of us has, even over natural inclinations and reactions to insults and injustice. Someone hurts us, we hurt back. Someone shouts at us, we shout back. What you don't realize is that by following this principle, you can be easily controlled because your reaction is so predictable.

Jesus teaches us to conduct our behavior according to our inner world (our spirit) of values, laws and principles rather than being controlled by external situations. These are principles, laws and values which exemplify the character of our true spiritual nature. Many of us are not at peace with ourselves because our outward behavior is not congruent with our true nature. This gives rise to inner conflict, guilt, low self-esteem, criticism, blame, depression, anxiety, timidity and many other negative emotions. We must realize that these are symptoms of the brokenness caused when our actions are diametrically opposed to our true nature.

Through self-control we can eradicate many of these negative emotions and live happy and fulfilling lives. As a matter of fact, happiness is determined by the degree of control that we have in any given situation. The more control we have, the happier we are. Anytime you are not happy, upon evaluation you will find it is because you lack of control over a situation.

Therefore the path to self control and true happiness is first found when you get in touch with your core values, beliefs and principles, and allow this to be the determining factor for all your decisions and conduct. This is the principle centered lifestyle. A principle centered lifestyle will attract into your life all that you desire which is congruent with what you value. Jesus puts it like this:

"IF YOU ABIDE IN ME AND MY WORDS ABIDE IN YOU, YOU WILL ASK WHAT YOU DESIRE, AND IT SHALL BE DONE FOR YOU" (JOHN 15:7)

ALSO
"...YOUR HEAVENLY FATHER KNOWS THAT YOU NEED ALL THESE THINGS. BUT SEEK FIRST THE KINGDOM OF GOD AND HIS RIGHTEOUSNESS AND ALL THESE THINGS SHALL BE ADDED TO YOU" (MATTHEW 6:32-33)

The kingdom of God is His way of doing things, His values and principles. Kingdom principles govern the universe and these principles work for anyone who puts them into practice, whether they believe in God or not.

If you study the lives of successful people, you will find that many of them practice what is in essence - Kingdom principles. For example, sowing and reaping, affirmations, goal setting and positive belief in the face of insurmountable obstacles. All of these are biblical teachings. Principle centered living enables you to live with integrity because your outward behavior will be consistent with your inner nature which in turn makes you whole. This is the very hallmark of integrity.

Principle centered living helps you to make decisions that will not take you away from your core values. If spending quality time with your family is one of your core values, accepting a job that pays well, but insists on long working hours will invite turmoil into your life. Principle centered living enables you to determine what you want out of life and the criteria for all achievements. This in turn gives you a great deal of control of your life as well as fulfillment.

Once you are clear about your core values and beliefs, the next step is to live responsibly. Responsibility is the acknowledgement of your influence in any given situation. Many people use blame to justify their inadequacies, experiences or lack of progress in life. Blame never solves problems; it only creates guilt, division and animosity. Blame allows us to play the role of the victim. Blame gives us justification for remaining exactly where we are for the rest our lives. How many of us still blame partners from past relationships for making our life miserable. How many of us are blaming our employers for us not getting promoted. How many of us are blaming our children for us not being able to pursue a career.

The truth is, we are responsible for what we experience in life. Please note that I did not say you are responsible for everything that happens to you, but for what you experience. What you experience is determined by the meaning you give to any given situation. Because meanings come under your sphere of influence, you are therefore responsible for what you experience. The reason why you are in a dead-end job, or a destructive relationship, or unemployed is because consciously or unconsciously, that is what you have chosen. As harsh as that statement sounds, it is also very liberating. If you are responsible for your own misery, then it stands to reason that you are responsible for your own happiness. Taking responsibility puts you in the seat of control. As a business owner, I take responsibility for everything that goes right or wrong within my sphere of control. If one of my staff fails to do something correctly, I ask myself, if I communicated what I wanted effectively? Have I provided the necessary tools to get the job done? Should I have fired this person months ago? Taking responsibility allows me to make the necessary changes for the better. If I blamed others when things go wrong, then I make no progress.

Many people have a great expectancy of their partner or spouse to provide their happiness. This can be a great burden as human beings by nature are not 100% reliable. Also this type of behavior depletes the relationship. Taking responsibility for your own happiness gives you a greater sense of security and self worth, which in turn helps you to add to the relationship and make it stronger. The next time you get angry with your wife, husband or partner ask yourself, *"What am I not doing in my life that I could be doing, that I am blaming him/her for not doing for me?"*

In taking responsibility, it is important not to blame yourself for past failures. It is a waste of your time and energy to punish yourself for past actions. If you adopt the attitude that each of us do the best we can according to our level of maturity and knowledge, you will stop blaming yourself. Instead, take responsibility by making sure you learn from your mistakes and gain the necessary experience or knowledge to aid your progress. As mentioned before, you are responsible for your reactions to any given situation. This may seem hard to believe until you understand what Stephen Covey calls the space of time between stimuli and response. In other words, there was a moment of time between someone 'cutting you off' whilst driving, and the volley of strong language that proceeded out of your mouth. It is in this moment of time that we can make decisions about how we are going to respond.

By becoming more self aware and staying in touch with your core values and beliefs, you will be able to widen the gap between stimuli and response and make choice decisions regarding your response. When tragedy hits your life, if your core belief is that God is able to deliver you from all afflictions, then you should not respond as if there is no hope. You have the power to choose your response and your attitude. Be yourself and do not copy the reactions of others. A bad situation does not justify discarding your core values and beliefs.

A principle centered lifestyle coupled with responsible living is the formula for achieving great fulfillment. Make the decision to eradicate every excuse or reason for not achieving your goals, by taking responsibility and therefore control of your life.

By taking control of your reactions, you have the ability to create a positive experience out of any situation. Remember that no one can make you do what you do not want to do. I will close with a quote from Ghandi:

"No body can take my self respect unless I give it to them"

◆PERSONAL POWER

INTEGRITY

The saying is sure and worthy of confidence: if we have died with Him, we shall also live with Him. If we endure, we shall also reign with Him. If we deny Him, He will also deny us. If we are faithless, He remains faithful; for He cannot deny Himself 2 Timothy 2: 11-13 paraphrased.

The opening text reveals that faithfulness is the very character of God and He cannot deny or act in any way that is inconsistent with His character. It is our character that distinguishes us and defines who we are. The way we react under different circumstances tells us of the quality of our character. How do we measure the

> INTEGRITY SITS ON THE THRONE OF HONESTY

quality of anything? Is it not by its ability to still function like new through the test of time and endurance. For example, iron and steel are both strong metals and in some cases can look the same externally, but under bad weather conditions or under pressure steel will prove to be stronger and more enduring. Another example is the difference between a gold watch and a gold plated replica of the same watch. At first appearance they may look the same, but when worn and exposed to the environment over a period of time, the gold plated watch will start to degenerate, even turn green in some cases.

In the same way the quality of a person's character is revealed, not when all conditions are favorable, but when exposed to challenges and unfavorable circumstances. God is faithful and He remains faithful to us even when we are faithless to Him (2 Timothy 2:13). This is what it is to have integrity. God wants us to be a people of quality. A person of quality bears the hallmark of integrity!

Merriam - Webster dictionary defines integrity as the state or quality of being entire or complete: wholeness, undivided and unbroken. The need for integrity is better known through an understanding of our true nature. We are in essence spiritual beings; therefore we must understand the nature of the spirit for this is our true character. The laws, principles and values taught in the Word of God, exemplify the character of the spirit that dwells within us. James illustrates this fact clearly:

"FOR IF ANYONE ONLY LISTENS TO THE WORD WITHOUT OBEYING IT AND BEING A DOER OF IT, HE IS LIKE A MAN WHO LOOKS CAREFULLY AT HIS NATURAL FACE IN A MIRROR; FOR HE THOUGHTFULLY OBSERVES HIMSELF, AND THEN GOES OFF AND PROMPTLY FORGETS WHAT HE WAS LIKE" (JAMES 1:23-24).

We can only be true to ourselves when we conduct our lives according to our spiritual character, as revealed in the Word of God. It takes integrity to be true to yourself. Without it there is no peace of mind! The Hebrew word for peace is shalowm. This word was used to denote completeness, soundness, health, prosperity and contentment. The phrase 'nothing missing, nothing broken' is synonymous with shalowm.

Can you see the similarity between shalowm and Merriam-Webster's definition of integrity? Integrity brings peace of mind and stability to our lives. So many of us are not at peace because our outward behavior is not in harmony with our true inward nature. This gives rise to inner conflict, guilt, low self esteem, blame, depression, anxiety, timidity and many other negative emotions.

Integrity begins with the mind

IF ANY OF YOU LACKS WISDOM, HE SHOULD ASK GOD, WHO GIVES GENEROUSLY TO ALL WITHOUT FINDING FAULT, AND IT WILL BE GIVEN TO HIM. BUT WHEN HE ASKS, HE MUST BELIEVE AND NOT DOUBT, BECAUSE HE WHO DOUBTS IS LIKE A WAVE OF THE SEA, BLOWN AND TOSSED BY THE WIND. THAT MAN SHOULD NOT THINK HE WILL RECEIVE ANYTHING FROM THE LORD; HE IS A DOUBLE-MINDED MAN, UNSTABLE IN ALL HE DOES. (JAMES 1:5-8 NIV).

The amplified version of the bible uses the term 'two minds' for double minded. At face value this term is used of someone who is indecisive, but a deeper understanding can be obtained when we understand the dynamics of the human mind. A comprehensive study of the mind is beyond the scope of this particular teaching but here are the basics. The mind is made up of conscious and subconscious functions. The conscious is responsible for comprehension, reason and conscious thought. The subconscious (biblically called the heart) is where core values, beliefs and assumptions are stored.

If integrity is at the helm of our mind, when it comes to our belief system, our conscious and subconscious should be in unity; acting as one mind. In other words, what I say with my mouth, I believe with my heart.

With this in mind, double mindedness is the state of

consciously speaking or thinking in a manner contrary to your subconscious beliefs and values. This condition is the very opposite to integrity and gives rise to hypocrisy. For example you may consciously state, "God is the great healer," but in your heart you believe that a particular disease is beyond God's ability. Thus, you show that you really do not have confidence in what you attest to be true. Confidence can only be achieved through integrity as it rests on the total belief (conscious and subconcious) in oneself or someone else.

Honesty v Fear

Integrity sits on the throne of honesty. Honesty with ourselves, honesty with others and especially honesty with God. The road to complete (inner and outer) healing begins with honesty. Often times being honest requires us to overcome our fears. Fear is the major stumbling block that prevents us from telling the truth. We experience fear when we consider what we might loose and the resulting pain associated with that loss. But God has not given us a spirit of fear; He has given unto us a spirit of love, power and a sound mind. Fear is a state of mind. It is the product of negative thought. Do not allow your mind to be controlled by fear. The bible gives an account of a woman who had been subject to bleeding for twelve years:

♦PERSONAL POWER

> Now a certain woman had a flow of blood for twelve years and had suffered many things from many physicians. She had spent all that she had and was no better, but rather grew worse. When she heard about Jesus, she came behind Him in the crowd and touched His garment. For she said, "If only I may touch His clothes, I shall be made well." Immediately the fountain of her blood was dried up, and she felt in her body that she was healed of the affliction. And Jesus, immediately knowing in Himself that power had gone out of Him, turned around in the crowd and said, "Who touched My clothes?" But His disciples said to Him, "You see the multitude thronging You, and You say, Who touched Me?" And He looked around to see her who had done this thing. But the woman, fearing and trembling, knowing what had happened to her, came and fell down before Him and told Him the whole truth. And He said to her, "Daughter, your faith has made you well. Go in peace, and be healed of your affliction" (Mark 5:25-34)

If there was anybody who had reason to be fearful, it was this woman with the issue of blood. First, she was a woman who lived in a society that in my opinion was not too kind to women - for example: the Pharisees brought a woman (before Jesus) who was caught in the act of adultery. They wanted to stone her. Did you notice who was missing? The man she was caught with! Anyway moving on, study shows the woman who suffered with this condition was probably married or betrothed. Her disease most likely would cause her husband to divorce her for the following reasons:

1. Because she would have been considered unclean and touching her husband would make him unclean

2. Sexual relationship would have been impossible or painful at the very least. This reason is likely because Jesus had to address a custom of men separating from their wives for no sound reason without giving them a certificate of divorcement.

Not only would she have faced the stigma of divorce and an embarrassing disease, but she would have been barred from the synagogue and public places because of her uncleanness. On top of that she had undergone all sorts of medical treatments that not only caused more pain, but also made her condition worse.

Imagine her having to uncover herself to many physicians with their primitive medical practices. She spent all she had trying to find a cure and now she was broke. She was desperate. She felt rejected and unloved. She was probably full of self-hate and anger. Angry at society, angry at men, angry at God.

Then at the lowest point of her life, she reached a turning point. She heard the reports of a man named Jesus. Jesus had healed many people of evil spirits and diseases in that area before. She certainly would've heard of Jesus healing the demoniac who lived just across the river, who was so possessed with demons that no chains could hold him. All of a sudden, something happened inside of her when she heard that Jesus had arrived.

Desperation turned into determination! She knew what she had to do and nothing was going to stop her from doing it. She overcame all her fears, all the social stigmas and taboos. The woman who was classed as an untouchable, pressed her way into the crowd - people she knew, people who despised her, people who felt she had no right to be there. She was focused and she was relentless. She was determined to reach her goal. And when her hand grasped the hem of Jesus' garment her faith connected with Jesus and power flowed from Him and the flow of blood from her womb ceased.

Not only was she healed by her faith, but also she was restored to health through her ability to overcome the fear of the stigma of her condition. Honesty is the key factor in exposing and addressing the root causes of problems in life. It takes courage to be honest in the face of adversity. It took courage for this woman to press into the crowd that surrounded Jesus and even more courage to tell Him the truth despite her fears. The lifestyle of integrity is not for the weak hearted but for the courageous.

Safe but not Sound

Often-times we are satisfied living with brokenness as long as we can anesthetize the symptoms. Vice such as pornography, alcohol, drugs and the like are at their core, various attempts to sedate the pain of brokenness and fill the void it creates. As long as we can continue with the daily grind of life, we settle for living broken. We strive to be safe but are not willing to go the extra mile to be sound. Safe and sound is not just an idiom, it speaks of two levels or stages of healing identified in the bible.

If we look at the story of the woman with an issue of blood again, we see that when Jesus discovered who had touched Him and heard her story, He said, "thy faith hath made thee whole; go in peace, and be whole of thy plague." If you study the text in the original Greek language you will find there are two different Greek words translated to the same English word WHOLE. The word 'whole' used in the woman's request for healing carries the Greek meaning for 'safe.' This pertains to health or relief from suffering and pain.

When Jesus said - "be WHOLE of thy plague", He was not just confirming what the woman had said in herself; He was using a different Greek word which meant 'sound'. This word sound meant complete, restored or whole in the fullest sense of the word.

✦PERSONAL POWER

So now, if we transliterate the words of Jesus we can see what really happened:

"YOUR FAITH RELIEVED YOU OF YOUR SUFFERING, NOW GO IN PEACE (NOTHING MISSING, NOTHING BROKEN) AND BE COMPLETELY HEALED AND RESTORED FROM YOUR DISEASE."

This woman who was so audacious in her quest, and had the opportunity to obtain total healing, took the safe option instead of the sound option. She had been through so much that all she wanted was relief from her disease, but not necessarily complete healing from her disease.

If Jesus had not looked for that woman, she would've been satisfied to walk away with only what she had. But what she had was not enough. We settle too easily for just getting by or scraping through. *Ordinary just won't do!* The standard that integrity demands is high only because you are a lot more than you think you are. If you do not seek to be whole (sound), no matter your status in life and no matter how much money you posses, you will always suffer from the pain of brokenness.

As I previously stated, the integrity-lifestyle is not for the weak hearted but for the courageous. Each of us have the potential of overcoming the greatest of challenges and being totally unstoppable through the power of God's Spirit that resides within us. It is vital that we discover our true nature rather than living according to human ideology.

Self discovery begins and ends through a Christ centered relationship with God. We were made in the image of God; therefore our true nature will only be revealed to us in the mirror of God's word.

◆PERSONAL POWER

DEVELOPING A SPIRIT OF EXCELLENCE

Be not conformed to this world; but be transformed by the renewing of your mind, that ye may prove what is that good, and acceptable and perfect will of God. Romans 12:2.

It is interesting that Paul urges us to be transformed rather than conform to the standards of the world. Webster's dictionary defines the word conform as coming into agreement or harmony, to be compliant or obedient or to act in accordance with prevailing customs. At face value this does not seem to be a bad thing. Why do

> EXCELLENCE IS THE HALLMARK OF SPIRITUALITY

we need to be transformed when we can just conform to the will of God? Can we not obtain the same results through compliance and obedience? In order to answer this question let us look at the word 'conform' again.

The word conform is made up of two words *con* and *form*. The word con is a prefix often used to denote opposition against something. The word form refers to the shape of a thing or structure. Therefore the word conform implies something being opposed or squeezed to fashion it from one shape to another, just like a potter fashioning a lump of clay into a vase by applying pressure with his hands. Conforming to God's way is like a potter taking that same clay vase, painting it gold and selling it as a pure gold vase. Although it may have the appearance of gold, it's true nature will quickly betray it.

Jesus paints a good illustration of the problem of trying to conform:

"NO ONE PUTS NEW WINE INTO OLD WINESKINS; IF HE DOES, THE WINE WILL BURST THE SKINS, AND THE WINE IS LOST AND THE BOTTLES DESTROYED; BUT NEW WINE IS TO BE PUT IN NEW (FRESH) WINESKINS" (MARK 2:22 - AMPLIFIED)

There is an expectation made by new wine that the old wineskin cannot meet. In like manner there is a standard the Word of God requires that cannot be met by our old way of thinking. A new and higher level of thinking is required which can only be achieved by the renewing of our minds. When I say 'higher level' of thinking, I do not mean a thinking which promotes self-righteousness. I am speaking of the kind of thinking that enables you to live more effectively and in harmony with the Kingdom principles that govern the universe. This is Kingdom thinking, which by nature is transformational, as it enables one to transcend any situation rather than being bound by it.

Transformation is a complete change of character and nature. It is like changing water into wine, clay into gold. Like the butterfly, we must be transformed in order to manifest our true beauty. In this context it is the transformation from one mindset to another. Paul identifies two types of people; the carnally minded and the spiritually (Kingdom) minded (Romans 8:4-8).

The carnal mind is only concerned with the physical life and places no priority on the quality of the inner life. The spiritually minded focuses on inner qualities, with the understanding that this is what influences life externally. By being spiritually minded we can begin to manifest our true and divine nature that has power to attract all that we would ever need into our lives. Therefore it is imperative that we have a clear understanding of what it is to be spiritually minded.

The best method of discovering the nature or purpose of something in the bible is to find where it is first mentioned (the law of first mention). The bible introduces The Spirit of God in His creative capacity. Therefore spirit by nature is creative. Through His Spirit, God creates in order to achieve His will. Achievement is the focal point of creativity. Nothing is achievable without creativity! Highly creative individuals constantly seek to push the boundaries of their work rather than resting on past achievements. They are always seeking new and better ways to advance themselves. That is why the bible says: *'the spiritual man tries all things [he examines, investigates, inquires into, questions and discerns all things]* – 1 Corinthians 2:15.

This state of constant advancement can be summed up in one word – excellence! Excellence is the hallmark of spirituality! Excellence is about constantly excelling oneself and improving on quality. It is important to note, that excellence starts from the inside out. In other words improving the quality of the mind is central to improving the quality of everything else.

One of the qualities of excellence is the attention to detail. Psalms 139:14 reveals that we were fearfully and wonderfully made, i.e., a great deal of thought and planning went into the creation of man. God is a God of excellence (Psalms 8:9). Excellence requires the ability to come out of your comfort zone and practice delayed gratification. Any high achiever will testify to this fact. The carnal mind is only concerned about comfort and instant gratification. A carnal minded person does not exhibit the mental qualities that a high achiever has. Thus the new wine of Kingdom principles would be wasted on a person whose thinking is purely carnal.

As mentioned, excellence requires renewing the quality of our minds. This is only possible when you are committed to your own personal development. Renewing your mind in a qualitative way is not a one-time event. It is a perpetual cycle of progress and improvement. Thus, excellence is an ongoing and infinite process. Never think you have arrived! There is always more to learn, always new ways of bettering yourself, always more to achieve.

So it is important that in the pursuit of excellence, we do not impede progress by trying to get everything perfect. They are many unfinished 'masterpieces' that may never see the light of day because of the obsession of trying to get it perfect. Perfection like excellence is an infinite process. The root word of excellence is excel and you can only excel on past achievements. The technology of today is far more superior to that of the last century. However, today's technology would not be what it is without the crude inventions of the past.

The path of excellence requires us to keep learning and keep creating. Learn more from what you have created and then create better. This is the cycle of excellence and the key to unleashing the unlimited potential that we all have. You must start from somewhere; so never despise humble beginnings, for it serves only as a seed that gives birth to greatness.

MORE THAN A CONQUEROR

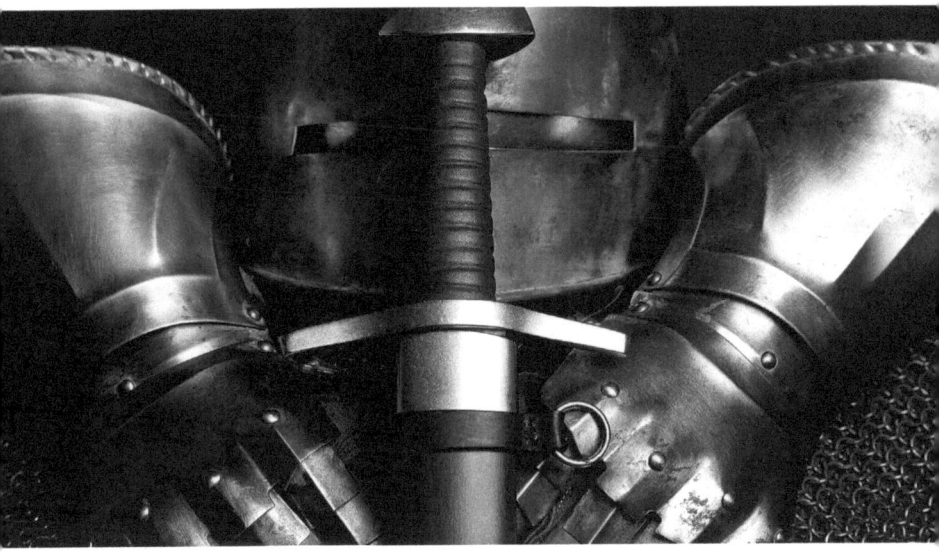

"We are more than conquerors and gain a surpassing victory through Him who loved us." Romans 8.37.

What does it means to be more than a conqueror? Is it not enough just to be a conqueror? If we look at the context in which this was written the writer (Paul) tells us not to let:

SUFFERING, AFFLICTION, CALAMITY, DISTRESS, PERSECUTION, HUNGER, DESTITUTION OR EVEN DEATH SEPARATE US FROM THE

> No weapon formed against you shall prosper

love of Christ. But even in the midst of these terrible things we are to be more than conquerors (Romans 8:35-37).

What does it take to be more than a conqueror?

Proverbs 16:32 says,

"He who is slow to anger is better than the mighty, he who rules his own spirit than he who takes a city."

Proverbs 25:28 teaches that the opposite is equally true,

"He who has no rule over his own spirit is like a city that is broken down and without walls."

A conqueror overcomes and controls an enemy or territory through military force. Being more than a conqueror requires rulership and control over over oneself. As Rudyard Kipling puts it so quaintly:

If you can keep your head when all about you
Are losing theirs and blaming it on you;
If you can trust yourself when all men doubt you,
But make allowance for their doubting too:
If you can wait and not be tired by waiting,
Or being lied about, don't deal in lies,
Or being hated, don't give way to hating,

And yet don't look too good, nor talk too wise;
If you can dream—and not make dreams your master;
If you can think—and not make thoughts your aim,
If you can meet with Triumph and Disaster
And treat those two impostors just the same:
If you can bear to hear the truth you've spoken
Twisted by knaves to make a trap for fools,
Or watch the things you gave your life to, broken,
And stoop and build 'em up with worn-out tools;

If you can make one heap of all your winnings
And risk it on one turn of pitch-and-toss,
And lose, and start again at your beginnings
And never breathe a word about your loss:
If you can force your heart and nerve and sinew
To serve your turn long after they are gone,
And so hold on when there is nothing in you
Except the Will which says to them: "Hold on!"

If you can talk with crowds and keep your virtue,
Or walk with Kings—nor lose the common touch,
If neither foes nor loving friends can hurt you,
If all men count with you, but none too much:
If you can fill the unforgiving minute
With sixty seconds' worth of distance run,
Yours is the Earth and everything that's in it,
And—which is more—you'll be a Man, my son!

IF by Rudyard Kipling (1895)

Anger

Life brings with it many challenges and often times we are thrust into situations seemingly beyond our control. The key to overcoming the challenges of life and even exercising power over circumstances, lies in the ability to maintain control over yourself and respond instead of react to any given situation. A response is the fruit of careful thought, whereas a reaction is action without thought. Anger (along with others) is a common reaction in times of trials and tribulation. If you are overwhelmed by anger you are no longer in control of yourself.

I have discovered two sources for anger. One comes from self-centerdness. When our prime concern is ourselves and yet we have not a true knowledge of ourselves, things said or done to us can be easily interpreted as insulting or offensive. This is because our ignorance about ourselves gives a foothold for insecurities, which stems from fear. I have found fear to be the motivating force for self-centerd anger. Examples of self-centerd anger are:

Volatile Anger
This type can easily be called 'unpredictable' or 'hair trigger' anger. In so many words, this type of anger comes and goes. Someone can be calm and collected

one minute, and be in a full rage the next minute. It can either grow into something bigger or go unnoticed. People who exhibit this anger tend to hold-in a large amount of things rather than expressing, in healthy ways, what may be bothering them. Seemingly meaningless actions or words can trigger of this anger. However, you will find the person is expressing anger from a past hurt rather than present actions.

Self-Inflicted Anger

This is a form of anger that is expressed when someone is punishing themselves for something they may have done wrong. Over-eating, starving themselves, and inflicting wounds by cutting themselves are examples of this kind of anger.

Judgmental Anger

This type of anger makes everyone involved feel uneasy or causes self esteem issues for the recipients. A person exhibiting this form of anger puts other people down and makes other people feel worthless as a person. However, you will find in every case that those exhibiting this type of anger either have serious self-esteem issues themselves or put down others in an effort to mask their own guilt. No wonder Jesus said *"Judge not, that you be not judged"* (Matthew 7:1).

The other source for anger is love. Anger expressed from love (zeal) is usually for reasons external to us, such as injustice (to others), or the desire to improve the lives of those living in poor conditions. Jesus displayed this when he drove the moneychangers out of the temple. He was consumed by zeal for His Father's house to be a house of prayer and not a house for merchandise (John 2:14-17). Many positive changes to people's lives have occurred through individuals who were angry enough to do something about it even at the cost of their own lives. Love based anger, although overwhelming, is always constructive and does not strip you of the ability to hold true to your core beliefs.

The key to More Than conquering

The ability to preserve your peace of mind in the midst of stormy situations is a greater feat than the ability to conquer a city. I am not saying that we are to conduct our lives oblivious to what is happening around us. Nor do I expect anyone not to be impacted by the blow life sometimes gives us. However, keeping your mind intact is an integral part of gaining the victory in any given situation. It must be said however, that victory is more than winning at the expense of your opponent's demise. Nor is about escaping difficult situations unscathed. You are truly victorious when you have come to the full realization that God is for you and not against you.

Battles you face are never faced alone:

AND WHEN THE SERVANT OF THE MAN OF GOD AROSE EARLY AND WENT OUT, THERE WAS AN ARMY, SURROUNDING THE CITY WITH HORSES AND CHARIOTS. AND HIS SERVANT SAID TO HIM, "ALAS, MY MASTER! WHAT SHALL WE DO?" SO HE ANSWERED, "DO NOT FEAR, FOR THOSE WHO ARE WITH US ARE MORE THAN THOSE WHO ARE WITH THEM." AND ELISHA PRAYED, AND SAID, "LORD, I PRAY, OPEN HIS EYES THAT HE MAY SEE." THEN THE LORD OPENED THE EYES OF THE YOUNG MAN, AND HE SAW. AND BEHOLD, THE MOUNTAIN WAS FULL OF HORSES AND CHARIOTS OF FIRE ALL AROUND ELISHA. SO WHEN THE SYRIANS CAME DOWN TO HIM, ELISHA PRAYED TO THE LORD, AND SAID, "STRIKE THIS PEOPLE, I PRAY, WITH BLINDNESS." AND HE STRUCK THEM WITH BLINDNESS ACCORDING TO THE WORD OF ELISHA (2 KINGS 6:15-18)

Like the servant of Elisha, your eyes need only to be opened to see that a host of resources, strategies and tools have already been put in place to secure your victory and vanquish the fears that debilitate your very being. In times of trouble, we do not need to resort to the primeval instincts which often result in being overwhelmed by anger, losing control or acting out of character. You are more than a conqueror when you realize that it stems from within and not without. Your mind is the spoil your enemy is after, not your possessions. Therefore you must guard your mind with the fortress of peace that can only be built with God's word. I will conclude with a powerful statement from the bible. Don't just see it as scripture or religious words to be desperately quoted in times of trouble. Let these words ripen your soul and transform your psychology:

No weapon formed against you shall prosper, And every tongue which rises against you in judgment You shall condemn. This is the heritage of the servants of the Lord, And their righteousness is from Me," Says the Lord (Isaiah 54:17).

FIT FOR ABUNDANCE

God is able to make all grace come to you in abundance, so that you may always and under all circumstance and whatever the need be self sufficient [possessing enough to require no aid or support and furnished in abundance for every good work and charitable donation]. 2 Corinthians 9:8 amplified

It is God's good pleasure for us to live successful and prosperous in every area of our lives. The question is - are you ready? Putting vast sums of money in the hands of someone who does not know how money works is like putting a loaded gun in a child's hand. You may have heard that money corrupts - well actually

Your money is not your own

money is an amplifier. It amplifies the character of the individual because financial freedom gives you access to what you never had before. If through financial freedom, you're now living a lifestyle of decadence, it is because decadence was in you in the first place. Money merely gave you the opportunity to express yourself. Knowing this, a person has to be found trustworthy in order for God to entrust them with abundant wealth. With the world facing economic melt down due to greed, sovereign debt and gross financial mishandling, you would understandably come to the conclusion that trustworthiness is clearly not a prerequisite for abundant wealth. However, if you want to have wealth as God wants you to have it, then trustworthiness is key. How does God want us to have wealth? He wants us to have and enjoy wealth with peace and no sorrow:

THE BLESSING OF THE LORD MAKES A PERSON RICH, AND HE ADDS NO SORROW WITH IT (PROVERBS 10:22)

The word trustworthy is translated *'faithfulness'* in the bible and is pivotal to wealth transfer in Jesus' parable of the talents found in Matthew 25:14-30. This parable provides profound insights into the kingdom dynamics of securing abundant wealth. We will look at this step by step and glean some of the principles this story offers.

FIT FOR ABUNDANCE

A MAN WAS ABOUT TO TAKE A LONG JOURNEY, AND HE CALLED HIS SERVANTS TOGETHER AND ENTRUSTED THEM WITH HIS PROPERTY. TO ONE HE GAVE FIVE TALENTS, TO ANOTHER TWO, TO ANOTHER ONE - TO EACH IN PROPORTION TO HIS OWN PERSONAL ABILITY. THEN HE DEPARTED AND LEFT THE COUNTRY. HE WHO HAD RECEIVED THE FIVE TALENTS WENT AT ONCE AND TRADED WITH THEM, AND HE GAINED FIVE TALENTS MORE. AND LIKEWISE HE WHO HAD RECEIVED THE TWO TALENTS - HE ALSO GAINED TWO TALENTS MORE. BUT HE WHO HAD RECEIVED THE ONE TALENT WENT AND DUG A HOLE IN THE GROUND AND HID HIS MASTER'S MONEY.

NOW AFTER A LONG TIME THE MASTER OF THOSE SERVANTS RETURNED AND SETTLED ACCOUNTS WITH THEM. AND HE WHO HAD RECEIVED THE FIVE TALENTS CAME AND BROUGHT HIM FIVE TALENTS MORE, SAYING, MASTER, YOU ENTRUSTED TO ME FIVE TALENTS; SEE, HERE I HAVE GAINED FIVE TALENTS MORE. HIS MASTER SAID TO HIM, WELL DONE, GOOD AND FAITHFUL SERVANT! YOU HAVE BEEN FAITHFUL AND TRUSTWORTHY OVER A LITTLE; I WILL PUT YOU IN CHARGE OF MUCH. ENTER INTO AND SHARE THE JOY WHICH YOUR MASTER ENJOYS (MATTHEW 25:14-21)

The first thing we must realize is that our money is not our own!

THE EARTH IS THE LORD'S, AND THE FULLNESS OF IT, THE WORLD AND THEY WHO DWELL IN IT - PSALM 24:1).

We are stewards of what belongs to God. A faithful steward is one who manages another's property, finances, or other affairs. Therefore he/she must adopt an attitude of accountability. God does not have a problem with

His money spent on ourselves; - but not all of it! Notice the master entrusted his property to his servants. The Greek rendering of the word entrust is made up of the words 'near' and 'give.'

There is a tendency to give what is valuable to those who are close to you. The people we should let close to us are those who have our best interest at heart. In like manner, God is looking for those whose hearts are for Him. Are you looking after God's interest or your own? Do you seek to advance and promote the Kingdom of God or your own?

Notice how the master diversified his money. It was not shared out equally, but according to the servants *personal abilities*. This indicates previous times when the master had entrusted them with either money or a special job, and based upon their individual performance, he could now accurately delegate varying levels of responsibility. It is obvious that the servant who received five talents had a proven track record of getting results.

Being trustworthy is not based on honesty alone, but also about being good at what you do. Hence the master called the five talent steward 'good and faithful'. This particular word 'good' in the Greek relates to *performance* and not morality. In other words "can you get results?" This is not due to natural talent, but a commitment to personal development. Being a faithful steward requires skill, not only in spiritual matters, but all aspects of life. Fortunately, the skills you need to get the desired results in life can all be *learned*. They have not been bestowed on only a few gifted individuals. You can learn about leadership, time management, money management, success laws, relating to others, business skills, communication skills, the list goes on. You can even learn to be confident! What about your health? Why should God entrust money into your hands when bad eating habits and lack of exercise encumbers your ability to perform. Make the decision to invest in yourself by learning the business of life:

THE WISE ALSO WILL HEAR AND INCREASE IN LEARNING AND THE PERSON OF UNDERSTANDING WILL ACQUIRE SKILL AND ATTAIN TO SOUND COUNSEL (PROVERBS 1:5)

DO NOT BE CONFORMED TO THIS WORLD, BUT BE TRANSFORMED BY THE RENEWING OF YOUR MIND, THAT YOU MAY PROVE WHAT IS THAT GOOD AND ACCEPTABLE AND PERFECT WILL OF GOD (ROMANS 12:2)

Renewing your mind is not a one-time event. It is a continuous cycle of advancing the quality of your mind. A word that defines this process is called 'excellence'. When excellence becomes the standard in your life, the words *ordinary* and *average* will be eliminated from your vocabulary.

As previously mentioned, the master gave the five talent steward more money than any of the others based on 'personal ability'. God is not a respecter of persons. He always operates according to the principle of His word rather than personal prejudices! God will give you more based on these principles:

"HE WHO IS FAITHFUL IN A VERY LITTLE THING IS FAITHFUL ALSO IN MUCH, AND HE WHO IS DISHONEST AND UNJUST IN A VERY LITTLE THING IS DISHONEST AND UNJUST ALSO IN MUCH" (LUKE 16:10).

"IF YOU HAVE NOT BEEN FAITHFUL IN THAT WHICH BELONGS TO ANOTHER WHO WILL GIVE YOU THAT WHICH IS YOUR OWN?" (LUKE 16:12).

Going back to the parable of the talents, we now understand the reaction of the master to the steward he had given one talent to. The one-talent steward was not faithful in that which did not belong to him; in fact, he had a poor attitude towards his master:

"I KNEW YOU TO BE A HARSH AND HARD MAN, REAPING WHERE YOU DID NOT SOW, AND GATHERING WHERE YOU HAD NOT WINNOWED" (MATTHEW 25:24)

Although I am a great advocator of entrepreneurship and owning your own business, having a job is a great opportunity for establishing the principles of stewardship in your life. Unfortunately, there are many who adopt the attitude of the one talent steward towards their employers. They do not like the fact that their employer reaps the benefits of their labour, and the thought of working over and beyond without extra pay is foreign to them. They would give only the minimum requirement their jobs calls for (sometimes below that). If this describes you, then you must realize your behavior is similar to the one-talent steward 'good-for-nothing!'

Just doing the minimum requirements of your job is like giving back the one talent you were given. Instead of seeing it as an opportunity, you treat it like an insult. You bury (withhold) your talent so your employer is not able to profit from his investment in you. You may argue that you are in a low pay job so why bother? But if you will not work with excellence in a low paid job, you will not work with excellence in a high paid job. Excellence should permeate every facet of your life.

Giving over and beyond what is required does not make you gullible. Instead, it increases your value to that company. At first, an employer may take advantage of this work ethic without extra benefit to you; but there will come a time (especially at the slight risk of losing you) when they will acknowledge you as a great asset to the company. Even if the company is going through financial difficulty and resort to shedding staff, in many cases they would get rid of staff that hold a higher position, but keep you. Many can testify to this.

Faithfully looking after that which does not belong to you will always increase your value to others. Adopting the attitude of owning the vision and mission of the company or organization you work for positions you for increase. Jesus puts it this way:

"I AM THE GOOD SHEPHERD. THE GOOD SHEPHERD RISKS AND LAYS DOWN HIS OWN LIFE FOR THE SHEEP. BUT THE HIRED SERVANT WHO IS NEITHER THE SHEPHERD NOR THE OWNER OF THE SHEEP, WHEN HE SEES THE WOLF COMING, DESERTS THE FLOCK AND RUNS AWAY. AND THE WOLF CHASES AND SNATCHES THEM AND SCATTERS THE FLOCK. NOW THE HIRELING FLEES BECAUSE HE MERELY SERVES FOR WAGES AND IS NOT HIMSELF CONCERNED ABOUT THE SHEEP" (JOHN 10:11-13)

So ask yourself this question - "are you a shepherd or a hireling?" As an employer, I would rather keep, train and invest in someone who is a shepherd, not a money motivated hireling.

If you are working for an employer who does not recognize your value, remember, promotion comes from above (Psalm 75:6). God is always looking out for those who will operate according to His principles and you will be rewarded in ways you did not think possible. Being faithful with that which does not belong to you goes beyond who you work for. Mismanagement of personal finances will certainly cause you to breach the principle of stewardship. Let me explain! The word 'manage' by definition means to regulate, control or organize. Achieving this involves a process of dividing something and assigning a function to each division.

For example, time management involves dividing your day into periods of time in which you perform specific or multiple tasks.

Many people fall into debt and financial trouble not because of low income but due to an unorganized method of spending and saving. They just spend as the need or desire arises. Good financial management starts with dividing up your income for specific uses. For example the first tenth (tithe) of our income belongs to God. Therefore if you receive an income but do not tithe you have breached the principle of stewardship by mismanaging what is not yours.

You can also breach the principle of stewardship by giving too much. Let me explain. Many times, in a church service or conference, we are asked to give a sacrificial offering. Because sacrifice is often associated with pain, there is a tendency for many to give more than they can afford, believing that God will give them more in return. The problem is, not all the money they gave belonged to them. They gave away what should have been set aside for gas, electricity, credit card repayment, the monthly installment for the new furniture and even the mortgage. Thus they have not been faithful with what was entrusted to them, even under the guise of giving to God. God honors the commitments you make to others even if you don't! We see this in Joshua 9 where the Gibeonites tricked Joshua into making a covenant of peace with them by pretending they were not from Canaan. Joshua's mission from God was to destroy all the inhabitants of Canaan. But now because of this covenant, he could not touch the Gibeonites without evoking the wrath of God.

You may think that dishonoring your commitments is ok because you are giving to God, but this is still untrue. In 1 Chronicles 21:18-24, David wanted Ornan to sell to him a plot of land where a threshing floor was located so he could build an altar and offer burnt sacrifices to the Lord. When Ornan offered it to him for free, David refused because he would not give to God that which did not *cost* him anything. David's conviction emphasizes the fact that what you give must belong to you, not others.

There are cases where the money you have will not cover your personal needs, let alone your financial commitments to others. In these cases it is essential that you sow [from] what little you have to fruitful ministries or organizations where the Lord's work is clearly evident. In so doing you will tap into the same principle as the widow of Zarepheth did, who, in the midst of a famine, gave Elijah the prophet a portion of her last meal first and (consequently) never ran out of food for the duration of the famine.

God loves a cheerful giver (2 Corinthians 9:7) and there

is nothing cheerful about 'giving until it hurts'. Also the purpose of sacrifice in a biblical context is dedication to the Lord. A sacrifice is what you dedicate to the Lord. The tithe is a tenth of your income dedicated to the Lord. When Paul beseeches us to present our bodies a 'living sacrifice' the emphasis is not to live a life of pain, but to dedicate our lives to the Lord. Although sacrifice is sometimes painful, it is your committed dedication to the Lord's will that shows your love for Him, not the (emotional) pain you endure.

With this in mind, we must practice good financial management where portions of our money are dedicated for a specific purpose. The practice of tithing is an important part of God's financial system, but what about the other 90 percent? The stewardship principle requires us to be faithful with 100 percent of the money that has been entrusted to us. God wants us to have the maximum benefit of the blessing he pours into our lives, instead of it being wasted. 1 Corinthians 10:13 reveals an underline principle regarding God's ability to give to us:

'NO TEMPTATION HAS OVERTAKEN YOU EXCEPT SUCH AS IS COMMON TO MAN; BUT GOD IS FAITHFUL, WHO WILL NOT ALLOW YOU TO BE TEMPTED BEYOND WHAT YOU ARE ABLE.'

The principle of this verse reveals that God does not allow us to have what we *cannot* handle. This principle of tithing is found in Malachi 3:10 NKJ

"BRING ALL THE TITHES INTO THE STOREHOUSE, THAT THERE MAYBE FOOD IN MY HOUSE AND TRY ME NOW IN THIS ," SAYS THE LORD OF HOSTS, "IF I WILL NOT OPEN FOR YOU THE WINDOWS OF HEAVEN AND POUR OUT FOR YOU SUCH BLESSING THAT THERE WILL NOT BE ROOM ENOUGH TO RECEIVE IT."

Tithing is an important part of God's financial system. However, it would be a mistake to believe that when you tithe, God is automatically obliged to bless your finances without you having to follow other biblical principles regarding economics. The principle of stewardship as it relates to personal finances requires faithfulness with all of the money that has been entrusted to you, not just a part of it.

In Malachi 3:10, God says He will pour out *for* us such a blessing that there will not be room enough to receive it. Notice He did not say He will pour a blessing 'on' us, but 'for' us. Therefore we must ask ourselves the question is - *where* will God pour His blessing for us? The answer is revealed in the following passages:

THE LORD SHALL COMMAND A BLESSING UPON YOU IN YOUR STOREHOUSE AND IN ALL THAT YOU UNDERTAKE (DEUTERONOMY 28:8)

HONOUR THE LORD WITH YOUR CAPITAL AND SUFFICIENCY AND WITH THE FIRSTFRUITS OF YOUR INCOME; SO SHALL YOUR storage places be filled with plenty, and your vats shall be overflowing with new wine (Proverbs 3:9-10)

God pours His blessing into storehouses! Storehouses are used to store things for future use. I am not suggesting that we each go and build barns so that God can bless us! A storehouse in a financial context is an organized financial structure that enables us to save, manage and use money effectively. Having revealed to Pharoah that there would be a famine in seven years, Joseph's advice gives a good illustration of how to use a storehouse.

"Now let Pharoah seek out and provide a man discreet, understanding, proficient, and wise and set him over the land of Egypt. Let Pharoah do this and appoint officers over the land, and take one fifth of the land of Egypt in the seven plenteous years. And let them gather all the food of these good years that are coming and lay up grain under the direction and authority of Pharoah, and let them retain food [in fortified granaries (storehouses)] in the cities. And that food shall be put in store for the country against the seven years of famine that are to come upon the land may not be ruin and cut off by the famine. And the plan seemed good in the eyes of Pharoah and in the eyes of all his servants (Genesis 41:33-37)

Joseph's advice prevented the death of millions of people. His storehouse plan represents a dynamic financial management plan. This plan serves as a vessel that God can pour into and bring multiplication into our lives. Let us examine his plan in detail.

Financial Intelligence
Seek out and provide a man discreet, understanding, proficient, and wise and set him over the land of Egypt.

Money is not everything, but everything involves money; therefore we must make it our duty to understand how money works and how to manage it. The subject of money is surrounded with controversy and taboos which has led to widespread financial ignorance and turmoil as most of the population struggle with mounting debt. However, there is no excuse for financial ignorance (or any sort of ignorance) with the wealth of information at our finger-tips through the internet or the numerous amount of simple to follow books written on the subject of finance.

Financial Planning
And the plan seemed good in the eyes of Pharoah and in the eyes of all his servants.

No planning is a plan for failure! Planning ahead gives us the ability to look into the future and see our desires fulfilled. God does everything according to His plan. There is nothing He does not have a plan for. Therefore we should adopt the same behavior with our lives. Your life goals will determine what your financial plan should be. Planning is our responsibility (Proverbs 16:1); however, we must present our plans to God so that they may be adjusted to fit and agree with His plan for our lives (Proverbs 16:3).

Financial Management
Appoint officers over the land, and take one fifth of the land of Egypt in the seven plenteous years. And let them gather all the food of these good years that are coming and lay up grain under the direction and authority of Pharoah, and let them retain food [in fortified granaries (storehouses)] in the cities.

Joseph appointed officers over the grain so that what was assigned for the granaries went to the granaries and what was to be sold was sold. As mentioned, financial difficulties occur not because of the lack of money but because of poor money management. Everything is spent according to immediate need or impulse rather than spending according to budget. A budget is a written plan in which you take your existing circumstances and financial goals into account – your current income and expenses. This is the most effective way to control your personal finances. From there, your budget becomes a plan of action by which you can get the maximum benefits from your existing income. It allows you to set priorities in regard to spending. Budgeting may not be the most anticipated activity on your family's agenda; however, it is a sure way to put into practice biblical principles of getting out of debt, saving and investing, sowing, tithing, giving to the needy and still be able to meet your basic family needs.

To aid you, create multiple bank accounts for specific purposes. For example, your giving account would have 10% percent of your income coming in from your salary account (preferably by standing order), for tithing, as well as money for donations. The amount for donations would be worked out according to your budget for other essential expenditure. From your giving account you can give donations to your hearts content; knowing there are no conflicts with other financial commitments or violation to the stewardship principle.

It is not the amount of money you earn that matters (many millionaires are in debt), rather it's how you manage what you have. The secret is living within your means. If you spend less than you make, you will always have a surplus. Unless you implement a budget, your expenses will invariably outpace your income. Budgeting allows you to develop control over your spending habits.

Saving & Investing
Take one fifth of the land of Egypt in the seven plenteous years.

A small surplus over time becomes abundance with the proper use of compound interest. If you spend less money than you take in, you will always have a surplus. Once you develop excess funds, you have the opportunity to make *money* work for you rather than you working for it. You should take control of your personal finances and never blindly leave them to someone else to handle. Banks and financial institutions create wealth by looking out for their interests first! The system is designed to work in their favor. Banks make money on the difference between what they pay you in interest on your savings and what they receive by investing your money.

In many cases, you can make the same investments for yourself and put the same income the bank would earn from your investments in your pocket instead of the institutions. Starting your own investment portfolio is not difficult and is not an exclusive club for an elite few. You will, however, need to get sound knowledge on the subject which is ready available through numerous training programs and easy-to-follow books on investing.

Become Solution Orientated

It was the gift of prophetic insight that enabled Joseph to save the nation of Egypt and the nations of the earth, from starvation. At the same time he brought great wealth and power to Egypt (and himself) because all countries went there to buy grain. Through prophetic insight Egypt had a monopoly on food and probably sold the grain at a higher price than usual.

A key insight to financial success is to understand that people only spend money on solutions! Look around your house, the table - the chair, a hair comb, food, curtains, paper clips, toothpaste, you name it, all that you bought was a solution to a problem, no matter how minor that problem. If you have anything that does not provide a solution, it is either junk or something you were duped into buying! Therefore, if you can clearly identify a problem and then provide a solution, you have what someone will pay for.

Although Joseph became wealthy through prophetic insight, money is not the goal or purpose for this gift. God created us with gifts and talents so that we can be a blessing to others. Those gifts are better utilized if we live a life of holiness. Unfortunately, holiness has been misinterpreted to mean 'better than thou or faultless.' The more accurate meaning for holiness is 'different' and 'unique.' God made us unique and in our uniqueness are solutions that the world needs. God does not want you to be a copycat. Instead He wants you to be an original, the way He intended you to be.

Remember this wealthy people do not work for money, they create it through:

* financial wisdom and winning strategies

* focusing on solutions

* providing solutions which are worth more to the customer than the cost of providing the benefit.

If you will make a commitment to listen and obey God in regards to His plan and purpose for your life, which draws on all the gifts and talent He has put inside you, success and prosperity will chase after you.

www.ingramcontent.com/pod-product-compliance
Lightning Source LLC
Chambersburg PA
CBHW042258280426
43661CB00097BA/1178